FUNDAMENTALS OF THE INTERROGATION TECHNIQUES

FUNDAMENTALS OF THE INTERROGATION TECHNIQUES

Satya Pratap Singh

KALPAZ PUBLICATIONS
DELHI-110052

Fundamentals of the Interrogation Techniques

Rs. 450

ISBN: 978-81-7835-716-4

Published in 2008 in India by
Kalpaz Publications
C-30, Satyawati Nagar,
Delhi-110052
E-mail: kalpaz@hotmail.com
Phone : 9212729499

Laser Type Setting by: Quick Media, Delhi
Printed at : Singhal Print Media, Delhi

KAUTILYA ON INTERROGATION

Kautilya warns us not to take a mere confession, without corroborative proof as proof of guilt; such confessions may be due to the fear of being tortured (4.8.11)

Dedicated to :

Dr. M.P. Singh, Ph.D
my elder brother, who taught me what to speak;
Dr. (Smt.) Mithlesh Singh, Ph.D
my wife, who taught me when to speak;
&
Shri M.L. Wadhawan,
former Member, Central Board of Excise & Customs &
Addl. Secretary Govt. of India
who taught me how to make a criminal speak.

Contents

Preface

There was one Mohammad Afzal from Pakistan. His entire family was killed in his native village owing to some dispute and a boy of fifteen years was the sole survivor. In a daring spirit of revenge at such a tender age he eliminated each and everyone responsible for the murder of his family members and crossed over to Amritsar district from Pakistan. He was eventually given shelter by few kind Sikhs of the village and since he was brought up by them they affectionately named him PALA SINGH.

In due course Pala Singh became a mountain of a man. Six feet four inches in height, weighing one hundred and twenty kilograms. He became a wrestler of repute but graduated to become a smuggler of gold of equal repute and assumed aliases of Pahalwan, Fazal Mohammad and Mohammad Afzal retaining Pala Singh as a mark of gratitude to those who brought him up.

I was fortunate to have him intercepted many times and get him detained under Conservation of Foreign Exchange and Prevention of Smuggling Activities Act. He had lot of respect for his physic and he never allowed any interrogator to touch his body but he was a man of convictions. He would narrate the entire sequence of events faithfully and request the interrogators to write it down as he did not know to read or write and had learnt only to sign his name in Hindi. He firmly believed that the law enforcing agencies should be respected and not cheated once one is caught. I met him last before his death in a court of law where I had appeared as a prosecution witness against him. He invited me for a dinner at his residence and understanding my hesitation in accepting the same politely stated that he had given up smuggling activities and was working as a contractor in fencing the Indo-Pak border. I was totally surprised and asked him as to how he had managed to bag the contract. With a mischievous smile he posed the counter question to me - was there any other person in India who knew Indo-Pak border better than him? I really had no answer. I wish I had accepted his invitation as it would have been a very fruitful interaction. It was way back in 1994. Interrogation of Pala Singh was a cake walk. He was an interrogator's delight. He would never conceal any facts however incriminating against him, before walking into Tihar Jail. Now let us witness the contrast in the year 2000.

Here are two young boys in their early thirties. One a Chartered Accountant by training and other with MBA degree from a prestigious University involved in a case of fraud and forgery of false exports of over 100 crores defrauding the national exchequer by way of over 30 crores, claiming false export incentives at Mumbai Port. After a prima facie case was made out, the honourable court remanded them to judicial custody for fourteen days with directions that they could be taken out from Jail for interrogation but should be lodged in jail by 5 p.m. on such day. Thus their interrogation were taken up while they were in judicial custody. To our amusement both of them would appear for interrogation with a book 'Constitution of India' and they even refused to write their own name quoting some Section of the Constitution. Obviously whenever the question of extension of judicial remand came up, we placed the copy of their statements before the Hon'ble Court, which took exception to their non-cooperation attitude bordering on contempt of court and the Magistrate went on extending their remand without counting the days beyond statutory limit of 60 days in the economic offences. This set an alarm in the syndicate and a senior advocate was flown from Delhi to Mumbai to get them enlarged on bail. On the day of hearing when it was a foregone conclusion that their judicial custody would be over and they will be released on bail, there were twenty one cars with garlands and bouquets in the Esplande Court to welcome them. Bail they did get, but by that time the Government had already issued their warrant of arrest for detention under the COFEPOSA and the Hon'ble Court was pleased to allow us to take them to Aurther Road Jail. All their petitions to get the detention orders quashed right up to the Supreme Court were of no avail. We continued their interrogation while they were in Preventive detention and realising the futility of their non-cooperational attitude, they later started singing like Canaries. If Pala Singh was a cake walk these two misguided youth were a nightmare. There is a vast, unchartered ground, full of landmines, between such diametrically opposite contingencies, which interrogator has to walk through in performance of his duties. It is here that the training, skill, experience, sound strategy and adequate preparation come into play. Sharing my experience with all humility is a small step in this direction.

The crime scenario all over the world has undergone sea change. The age old adage that Zar, Zoru and Zamin (Money, Women and Land) are the only root cause of a crime, although still valid and shall remain relevant till man inhabits the earth, does not encompass the wide ranging criminal activities of a pervert mind of modern age. Religious fundamentalism, unbridled lust for wealth, terrorist activities, et al have added new dimensions to the current crime-scenario. These criminal activities are offences against humanity at large and the society and a nation suffers at the hands of certain misguided elements of the society. Smuggling activities drain away the genuine wealth of a nation and a financially sick nation struggles to protect its existence amid highly materialistic and competitive member nations. Religious fundamentalist and terrorist activities where on one hand demolish the well harmonised social structure on the other hand bring untold miseries, death and destruction to others who are in no way responsible whatsoever to undergo such sufferings. Law enforcing agencies are thus incessantly engaged to combat these individuals or group of individuals who perpetrated the crime for their myopic philosophy or greed for money. Crime investigation therefore assumes unimaginable significance for stability of harmonious social order and rule of law. Although there are innumerable tools and aids available in the detection of crimes but there is no substitute for a human mind. Latest gadgetry may, at best, put us on the right track because equipments can only show us the way but can not speak. We have to make the criminal speak to take a case to a logical end to ensure his conviction hence the techniques of interrogation call for a fresh, unbiased and holistic approach so that the criminal cooperates in reconstructing the crime scenario.

Interrogation is a technique which does not come all of a sudden. In fact with each case personality of the interrogator undergoes an evolving process which helps one in honing the skills. Third degree methods only spoil the case as well as the interrogator. Under coercion one may speak what an interrogator wants him to, but any seasoned and skilled lawyer will pierce through the glaring holes of the fabricated story of the prosecution and demolish the whole case during the cross-examination in a court of law. Upper most point in any interrogator's mind should therefore be faithful reconstruction of a crime which should not only be credible, faithful to the facts but should also be able to withstand the microscopic scrutiny of the court.

Our problems of interrogation have further compounded. Ms. Olga, a conduit of smuggling syndicate which may be a cover for nefarious activities does not know the languages we speak. An Al Qaeda or Hizbul Mujahideen will also fall in the same category. Similar dilemma we come across in identifying illegal migrants of the Bangladesh owing to plethora of dialects spoken by them. It will be a daunting task to reach their minds owing to language barriers and we have to have a person well conversant with the nuances of language to assist us. In present scenario we will get far too many criminals who even though trained to communicate in lingua franca of their country of operation, will feign not to understand our questions and evade successfully the in-depth investigation.

There are certain prerequisites to become a good interrogator and these qualities should be imbibed by those designated to handle such jobs. In fact these should be so ingrained that these become a permanent feature of our mind set. First and foremost is the patience. We tend to have no patience and no sooner an alleged accused is intercepted the process of interrogation is set in motion beginning with good thrashing, like a bollywood masala film hero with complete disregard to time and place. Every one pounces on the target and starts shooting question like a cloud burst. Such outburst may be owing to long drawn out surveillance operations nevertheless it should be discouraged. The accused gets an inkling of what is in store for him and he immediately judges your line of investigation like a good cricket batsman and sets in defense mechanism in process the moment ball is released by the bowler. Every criminal when he is in hiding and absconding he is constantly aware of his problem and mentally prepares to overcome the ordeal. Some may be highly indoctrinated and motivated and any caviler fashion approach should be judiciously avoided.

Perseverance is another pre-requisite. The accused is bound to float various stories to misguide you. Perseverance can best be achieved if one is a good listener. Listening is an art, and an act of silence, when the mind is quiet but tremendously active and you would not fall into pit or be inclined to purchase a false and incredible story. One should never get tired of listening and the accused should be encouraged to speak as much as possible making him vulnerable to his own inconsistencies. After a marathon session you can simply say "I do not believe it, tell me the truth", the accused is again back to square zero and starts all over again with something new which may be less plausible story and in sheer exasperation will eventually come out with true facts. Even if the resistance is still continuing there will be large gaping holes in the alibi being sold out to enable you to penetrate his defenses when he ultimately give up.

Persistence is yet another vital component of a good interrogator's personality. It is often seen that we give up more easily than the accused. Never be in a hurry and always persist in your effort till the truth has finally come out. This is most problematic area because we are really swimming against the current. The statutory requirement of producing an accused in a court of law within twenty four hours has to be adhered to. Human right activist, battery of lawyers, friends and relatives hover around the office and hamper the investigation by their irritant behavior. Even if we have safe houses some are of not much help because the media too chips in and flash stories, which are definitely prejudicial to the public interest. Courts are also not very much inclined to grant police remand and prefer judicial remands. All these factors are like speed breakers and have to be negotiated skillfully. The profile of the present day criminal is diametrically opposite to the criminals of the past. I am talking about the leaders of the perpetrators of crime, who are highly educated, articulate, accomplished having nexus to the right places and persons and to elicit confessions within twenty four hours is really a nightmare. Legal stipulation however has to be scrupulously honored and this brings us to the fourth requisite and that is training.

Training is most neglected part of our law enforcement system. People do not prefer to go on training unless it is more lucrative than where one is currently posted. Offer a training assignment in London or New York and the whole department will volunteer. More than training, it is the sight seeing which is the motivating factor. With such attitude the right person has a very little chance to be nominated.

Besides, when such persons come back after training they are never assigned the job for which they have gone abroad and rightly so because it is assumed he may not have learnt anything during the training. Even for those assignments which are available in the country person whose home town is close to the training institute grabs the chance. Even local holiday is not an inferior consolation. You would not be surprised to find a Hindi speaking officer proceeding to do a course in Hindi all the way from Mumbai to Delhi. It may seem strange nevertheless true that the right person is seldom spared for a training course because his services cannot be dispensed with. During the course of my service we did succeed in roping in IB, RAW and Military intelligence school to train officers from the revenue department but it was more because of personal equations and rapport than any institutional working arrangement. But even these institutions can fulfill limited role. In fact personnel from all law enforcing departments require intensive training in banking operations, chartered accountancy and share market functioning. Unfortunately training in these institutes is highly costly and sponsoring departments have no funds for such contingencies because it was never considered a necessity in the past.

A criminal today has no respect for geographical or political boundaries. A foreign mercenary acting as an ISI operative may land into the net of an agency in Coimbatore in Tamil Nadu or in Aizwal in Mizoram. Even to have preliminary profile of the criminal we have to avail the services of an interpreter. A bridge has to be constructed between the interrogator and the alleged accused and there is no substitute to the knowledge of language which a criminal understands. It is very demanding requirement since we can not afford to have workforce of linguists idling away their time in the hope of getting a criminal to talk to. We have nevertheless fair idea as to what type of suspect we are likely to get in near future and with such foreknowledge a panel of interpreters can be constituted to be available at short notice. Empanelling should be done very carefully and persons so selected should be of unquestionable integrity. In fact an interpreter's role assumes more significance than that of interrogator because an interpreter ipso facto performs the functions of the interrogator.

When we talk of the role of an interpreter how can we forget the body language of the accused. After all what is a lie detector. It only interprets the body language. In contrast study of body language by an interrogator is more effective because he can simultaneously rise to the occasion and formulate his strategies. The most visible signs of body language are manifest at the time of interception. An accused is bound to get stunned. Nervous may sweat, become breathless. He may even become motionless like a hypnotized rabbit. It all depends how carefully and skillfully the interception has been executed. Lightening interception with total element of surprise is bound to derail any hard criminal and study of his body language at this critical moment is like striking at a treasure house because the accused displays the weakest facets of his personality at this juncture. Video recording of these events can act as permanent background material and will serve as a valuable record for future as well. In fact during the presentation of department's case before the Advisory Board of the Hon'ble Delhi High Court in a COFEPOSA matter we were asked as to why we were not video recording our dramatic interceptions of the smugglers. We thought the question was posed to us in the lighter vein. In retrospect, it is realized now that besides crucial evidential value such video clippings can prove to be very effective tool in the art of interrogation.

Interrogation is a very complex task. There can not be rigid guidelines since essentially it is battle of wits between two minds; one trying to conceal, other in the pursuit of unearthing the same. I cannot restrain from citing a short story which is very much relevant to our problem. In a village there were two farmers, the first one called Alfa was cultivating onions and other named Bravo was engaged in cultivation of garlic. Both were living in stark poverty as the yield was not giving them the returns sufficient to sustain the life. One of them decided to visit the neighboring king with a view to sell his product in the hope of getting rich returns. He presented himself in the Durbar of the King with a bag of onions and pleaded with the king to purchase the same. The king had never heard of onion but laid the condition that he would purchase it and if it did not satisfy his taste he would get the farmer beheaded. Poor farmer agreed as he was confident of himself. On the following day, as the king was mighty pleased awarded him with gold coins of equal weight. On seeing that the lady luck had been so generous to Alfa, Bravo also tried the same trick with the King. Similar conditions were imposed on him as well by the king. Obviously, the king was more pleased with the garlics and on the following day announced in the open Durbar that the farmer deserves to be awarded with more precious thing than gold and ordered that onions of equal weight be given to the farmer. Totally dejected Bravo returned to his village and resigned himself to the life in the same old cruel poverty. The moral of the story is that an interrogator like the onion seller instead of being stereotyped or imitator has to be confident, focused, determined and prepared to take the risk, as things do not come in a platter. An interrogator has to be imaginative, innovative and confident of his approach, since beaten tracks do not necessarily take one to the intended destination. One had to carve out his own path and handle the situation without influence of prejudicial inhibitions.

Quality of interrogation is yet another hallmark of investigator's personality. In working out a case, a large number of persons may be interrogated and intensity of questioning will differ from individual to individual and has to be formulated within the broad parameters of the overall strategy. Number of pages written by the accused or the hours he was grilled is really not of much consequence. Even one liner interrogations can also yield miraculous results. There was a person, let us call him Charlie, who was the leader of notorious syndicate specializing in false exports by forging the documents and had laundered few hundred crores by his nefarious modus operandi. Few hundred crores had been pumped in against his exports through banking channels and the most alarming aspect of his operation was that all his activities were abated by one notorious smuggler of Pakistan based at Dubai. It could be safely inferred that his Principal's in Dubai could be a covert ISI operative. Charlie planned his operations very meticulously. He would never do anything personally, never sign any documents with the results be never left any trail behind, of course he had the services of young and unemployed youth having Chartered Accountant and MBA degrees from reputed universities. Apparently the inducements were very high and such misguided youth fell into his trap. Charlie was duping the investigating agencies since 1993 and although he was arrested number of times but come out from jail for lack of evidence. He not only amassed wealth but developed clout in right places to laugh at the law of the land. He acquired so much importance that he always went around with gunman from Police for his personal safety. Now imagine who would give corroborative evidence against such high profile criminal. So I decided to summon him for interrogation.

Against my expectations he did appear before me at the appointed hour and date. So confident was he of himself and so offending in his arrogance that instead I interrogate him he started interrogating me. He vehemently opposed my idea of summoning him as according to him it was not my job and should be left to some junior officers. I coolly asked him whether he had viewed the famous serial *Ramayana* on the television. Religious man as he was, having astrology as his front operations for living, the answer was in positive. My next natural question was as to who had killed demi-God Ravana? Monkey God Hanuman or Laxman? He looked at me with contempt and fast came the reply that it was Lord Rama who killed Ravana. I politely informed Mr. Charlie that his interrogation was over and he was at liberty to go. It completely shattered his confidence. His syndicate members deserted him, came forward voluntarily to speak about his nefarious activities which ultimately resulted in his Preventive detention for one year besides other members of the syndicate. But he was not to give in easily and went underground to evade arrest. Detention was challenged in the High Court by way of a writ petition which the Hon'ble Judges dismissed. A solemn assurance was given to the Hon'ble High Court that the detenu will surrender on a auspicious day which never came. Ultimately he was nabbed by the ever inspiring sleuths of the department from his den from a housing society complex inhabited by top film stars of the industry in Lokhandwala complex in Mumbai. Needless to say three get away cars parked at different places for a smooth get away was of no help to him since all escape routes was already sealed. Although Charlie did not honour his commitment to the Hon'ble Court, the department therefore in ironic deference to his wishes apprehended him only on Mahashivratri day.

Few anecdotes and live cases have been shared only to emphasis the importance of interrogation which is very crucial to obtain a confession of irrefutable evidential value in a court of law. An unbiased approach, patience and diligent work are perquisites to uphold the spirit of the law and consequently very detrimental to criminal activities. All facets of interrogation are being capsuled into following chapters and in the end synopsis of certain difficult cases is appended at annexure to demonstrate as to how the break-through was achieved.

(i) Economic crime scenario in India

(ii) Infrastructure

(iii) Curtain raises

(iv) Techniques of Interrogation

(v) Modern scientific aids in interrogation

(vi) Interrogation and Intelligence gathering

(vii) Interrogation and vulnerability of a criminal

(viii) Joint Interrogation

(ix) Faulty Interrogation and comedy of errors

The cases, which have been illustrated in Part-II, primarily pertain to economic offences. These were really tough cases to crack but ultimately solved by adopting certain unorthodox methodology. Usually no two cases are identical, unless same set of criminals and similar objective is their intention, in which case a pattern of modus operandi may emerge. It is therefore, imperative that each case be viewed with unbiased standpoint to achieve objectivity and purposeful results.

I am indeed grateful to Shri P.K. Dash, a colleague of mine, Secretary (Trade) at Brussels, for his immensely valuable suggestions in my efforts. Special thanks to my son Dr. Sharad Chauhan, I.P.S., and Smt. Vishal Chauhan, my daughter-in-law for persistently motivating me to reduce my experiences in writing.

Introduction

The art of interrogation goes to the very crux of what lies ahead as far as the criminal judicial process is concerned. It is at the vital point of time when the interrogation is being carried out that the whole case is made out; all the material facts that the enforcing authorities seek to rely on are revealed, and it is crucial that any flaws or holes in the story are caught in time, so as to prevent a lawyer from exposing these in cross-examination.

In this book, Shri Satya Pratap Singh has gone into the understanding of how to carry out interrogations, ensuring that the credibility of what is revealed is kept intact and will be able to withstand the examination of the courts. Enumerating of the most significant factors and characteristics that make an interrogator more efficient at extracting information, he suggest one employ some of following - patience, perseverance, persistence, dedicated training, fluency in more than one language, and understanding body language, among other things.

With references to his personal experiences, and sharing his own practical applications of these skills, he lays out several positive and effective guidelines that I am sure will help law enforcement officers and forces throughout the country.

I wish him every success.

R.K. Anand

PART–I

1

Economic Crimes Scenario in India

I had a very promising Brigadier friend who could not make it to the higher echelons in the Army owing to his untimely by pass surgery. He had two sons and one of them joined the Indian Navy while the other opted for the Army. I ventured to ask him once as to why he persuaded the other son to join the army instead of any other force without blinking his eyes he said that the real joy of soldiering is derived when you kill the enemy face to face and that privilege you could get only in the army, whereas Navy or Airforce relies more on stealth in destroying the enemy after spotting the same on the radar screen. Typical answer, but very true too. The modern crime scenario also relies heavily on secrecy, stealth and deceit and the impact is known when enough damage is done and it is too late. Be it suicide bombing of World Trade Towers in the States or back home, the UTI scam or non-payment of banking loans, where thousands of crores have gone down the drain owing to ingenuity and manipulative techniques. By the time, the gravity of these offences was unfolded, it was really too late as the damage was already done.

With the rapid advancements in the science and technology and shrinking of geographical boundaries, the world has come closer and there is quantum leap in the financial transactions the world over by way of international trade, industrial developments and other sectors of the economy. Apparently, it gave new dimensions to the economic crimes across the globe. The crisis in governance is too manifest as we see the enactment of various Statues by the Legislatures from time to time since the Indian Penal Code, which was once sufficient to tackle any crime is currently grossly inadequate. Though it may be extremely difficult to have an exhaustive list of all types of white-collar crimes but the following list would give sufficient indication as to how difficult the job of an interrogator has become now.

(i) Smuggling
(ii) Exchange Control violations and illegal currency smuggling
(iii) Counterfeiting of currency and valuable negotiable documents
(iv) Forgery
(v) Corporate frauds
(vi) Fraudulent insurance claims
(vii) Social Security and Welfare frauds
(viii) Security frauds like issuance of worthless stock, market manipulation and insider trading
(ix) Illegal restrictive practices and monopolies
(x) Banking frauds
(xi) Shipping frauds
(xii) Credit frauds
(xiii) Credit Card frauds
(xiv) Economic and Industrial espionage
(xv) Bribery
(xvi) Corruption
(xvii) Tax Evasion
(xviii) Pirating of films, publications, etc.
(xix) Copy right and Trade mark violation
(xx) Frauds relating to bankruptcy and insolvency
(xxi) Falsification of accounts
(xxii) Money laundering
(xxiii) Terrorist funding

These various crimes overlap each other. Certain crimes are precursor to even more serious crimes; for example, tainted money generated through illegal narcotics trade is invariably used for terrorist funding, buying of arms, ammunition and explosives. In one of our neighboring country, the situation is so grave that the civil police is so helpless that to search the Drug Mafia strongholds, army's help is sought invariably.

In our country no scientific study has been ever undertaken to study the trend of crimes, its magnitude, impact and its shape to come, so much so that to learn that we are one of the most corrupt nations we have to look for a report published by a foreign agency. We have been in fact treating white-collar crimes like diabetes. Once the blood sugar level is restored to out of danger limits, we go to sleep no wonder we are perpetually embarrassed by one scam after the other.

Whereas all white crimes may not be so damaging because those may be isolated cases perpetrated by an individual say, for example, cheating or forgery, but whenever any white-collar crime generates from the criminal conspiracy of group of individuals, syndicates and organizations, then the ramifications are far too damaging, at times irreparable and may even erode the economic fabric of the society and faith in the market economy. Certain white -collar crimes not only destroy the economic and social fabric of the society but also impose a very heavy burden on the interrogators to unearth the leads, modus-operandi, leadership and above all evidence to bring them to justice.

With a view to have an overview of the economic crime scenario in India sample study of major economic crimes is imperative and we would dwell on the following economic criminal activities.

I. Trafficking and Abuse of Narcotic Drugs and Psychotropic Substances

The menace of drug trafficking and its abuse has assumed serious proportions as the same is not only damaging the socio-economic fabric of the society but is also being extensively used for generating tainted money with a view to generate funds for clandestine activities in destabilizing the political system in a country. India, sandwiched between the 'golden triangle' and 'golden crescent' on our neighborhood is strategically located which is very conducive for smuggling of the narcotic drugs and psychotropic substances.

Afghanistan on our north-west, has acquired notoriety in illicit cultivation of Opium and as per informed estimates approximately 450 Tons of Heroin is produced annually illegally, which worth about US $ 90 billion. Obviously, the huge funds raised from illicit trafficking of the drugs could be used for promoting international terrorism. Keeping in view the seriousness of the problem it needs no emphasis that the menace of drug trafficking requires holistic approach by all the nations in the world and also international co-operation to curb the menace, if not, eliminate altogether. We have to tackle this problem at the statutory level, evolve enforcement machinery backed with legal sanctions and skillfully trained manpower to tackle the same. At the same time, mass education programme also have to be undertaken by governmental agencies and also non-governmental organizations to ensure the reduction in the demand of the narcotic drugs and psychotropic substances by its users.

National Policy of India on Narcotics Drugs and Psychotropic Substances is based on the Directive Principles enshrined in the Constitution of India. Article 47 of the Indian Constitution casts an obligation on the state to endeavor to bring about the prohibition, except for medicinal purposes, of intoxicating drugs injurious to health. It is in the implementation of this constitutional imperative and in recognition of the danger that drug trafficking represents for humanity at large, the anti-narcotics laws were consistently upgraded, and for effective control of drug menace Narcotic Drugs and Psychotropic Substances Act 1985 was enacted, the act was further amended in 1989 incorporating stringent provisions like forfeiture of property of the dealers.

Simultaneously for strengthening the operations for combating the drug menace, Narcotics Control Bureau was established as an apex body, for coordinating the efforts of various organizations at national and international level. Also along with the police, the officers of Revenue agencies such as Central Excise and Customs, Border Security Forces were empowered under the NDPS Act 1985. Narcotic Cells were established in each Commissionerates of Central Excise and Customs. These cells are effectively combating the illicit trading in Narcotic Drugs and Psychotropic Substances.

Drug Scenario in India

The problem of drugs in India is a mix of a number of factors. These are India's geographical location between two major opiate producing regions in South West and South East Asia; the inherent dangers of leakage from India's licit opium crop; the wild and illicit growth of the opium poppy and the cannabis plant in certain parts of the country, the inflow of cannabis resin and marijuana from Nepal, and the fact that India has a highly developed chemicals industry which manufactures some of the precursors listed in the 1988 UN Convention against illicit trafficking in Narcotics Drugs and Psychotropic Substances. Methaqualone trafficking and clandestine laboratories for the manufacture of Mandrax also constitute a significant concern.

Drug Law Enforcement in India consequently confronts the problems of transit, particularly of South West Asian heroin, as well as of domestic consumption, trafficking and export. Heroin sourced from South East Asia, though not trafficked through India, increasingly caters to the burgeoning demand in our North Eastern States. Precursor control must strike a balance between the imperative of preventing diversion and the legitimate interests of trade and industry.

Strategy and Policy

The Narcotic Drugs and Psychotropic Substances Act, 1985 sets out the statutory framework for drugs control in India. This Act consolidates the erstwhile principal Acts viz. The Opium Act, 1957, the Opium Act, 1878 and the Dangerous Drugs Act, 1930 and also incorporates provisions designed to implement India's obligations under various International Conventions. Certain significant amendments were made in the Act in 1989 to provide for the forfeiture of property derived from drugs trafficking and for control over chemicals and substances used in the manufacture of Narcotics drugs and Psychotropic substances. In order to give effect to the statutory provisions relating to "Controlled Substances", an order namely the NDPS (Regulation of Controlled Substances) Order was promulgated by the Government of India in 1993 to control, regulate, and monitor, the manufacture, distribution, import, export, transportation etc. of any substance which Government may declare to be a 'controlled substance' for the purposes of the Act. The statutory regime in India consequently encompasses drugs trafficking, the assets derived from drugs trafficking and also substances which may be used in the manufacture of Narcotic drugs and Psychotropic substances.

India has evolved a multi-dimensional drugs control strategy targeting both supply control and demand reduction. As a number of agencies, both at the Centre and in the States are involved in combating drugs, appropriate mechanisms have been evolved both at the policy and at the operational levels in order to optimize the efficacy of the resources committed to this task. These mechanisms consist of an apex level. Coordination Committee of the Union Secretaries of Revenue, Home, Health and Social Justice and Empowerment which addresses questions of policy, and operational national level coordination between Central and State agencies through structural interactions between the Director General, NCB and the heads of these Agencies. State and regional level coordination is also maintained through regular meetings between the concerned officials. For a detailed profile of the Drug Law Enforcement in India, please see Appendix-A .

II. Outright Smuggling of Gold and Other High Price Commodities

Although the difference in prices of the gold in India and major gold producing trading countries abroad has been the major factor of cause of smuggling of gold in to India but the additional cause of lure for the yellow metal has been its stability in fluctuating economy resulting into security of investment. Today, when the confidence of the investor is badly shaken because of various financial scams, gold continues to be the safe haven for investment owing to its price stability, as can be seen from the prices of the yellow metal in the London Metal Market during the last century (Please see Appendix-B). The price trend of gold in India has more or less been echoing the world prices of gold. (Please see Appendix-C). Gold also continues to be a reliable mode of payment against smuggling of narcotic substances. Besides gold, arms and ammunition, explosives, bearings, silk yarn and electronic goods are other lucrative items since these fetch very high margin of profit in the local market. In fact, there has been unprecedented spurt in smuggling of electronic items from China, in the recent years. The seizure figures on all India basis for the last two years (Please see Appendix-D) indicates the menace of smuggling. These statistics, at best, only reveal the tip of the iceberg, as our experience suggests that with the best of our efforts only small percentage (around 10%) of the total contraband smuggled is seized in the country.

III. Revenue Frauds

In addition to outright smuggling cases, our economy is also plagued by numerous tax frauds, which pose more serious threat than outright smuggling. It is in this sphere of crime that highly educated and economically well-placed syndicates/individuals are involved. Loopholes of the law are blatantly exploited to circumvent the law to become rich overnight. Secrecy, stealth and speed are the key factors for nefarious syndicates to flourish. Add to this stamina factor generated by these groups owing to bureaucratic or political clout, these groups are detected when sufficient harm has already been done to economy. Some of these frauds could be listed below :-

(a) Valuation fraud. The valuation fraud is a major problem among many World Customs Organisation Member nations that are creating serious dents into the social, economic and political fabrics of a nation. Although, it is a known fact that any individual or a firm undertakes a business activity primarily with a view of profit incentive, however, in the present global scenario there seems to be more than exclusive monetary consideration.

As we are all aware that with modern developments in the science and technology, the entire globe is now reduced to a global village. The world has shrunk owing to fast travel and communication systems and therefore what happens in one part of the world has direct bearing on other nations as well. The most disturbing phenomena in global political scenario are emergence of religious fundamentalism, ethnic violence, drug trafficking and host of other crimes that require clandestine funding. It may be true in some cases that these activities are promoted at times with legitimate money but in most cases bonafide trade transactions like imports and exports are also being used as a conduit to raise funds for undertaking nefarious activities. It is in this context that the valuation frauds assume paramount importance and the problem has to be addressed in right earnest. The problem has assumed such alarming proportions that even United States of America feels insecure from the onslaught.

(b) Misuse of DEEC Scheme. The Duty Exemption Entitlement Certificate (DEEC) scheme continues to be misused by unscrupulous elements. Violations of the DEEC Scheme have ranged from outright diversion of duty free imported goods, without the export obligations being fulfilled, to misdeclaration and over-invoicing of export goods. The exporters resort to this to fraudulently claim fulfilment of export obligation. Under invoicing is resorted to in respect of imported goods with a view to import more quantity within the value of the licence.

(c) Misuse of DEPB Scheme. Specific cases of misuse of Duty Entitlement Pass Book (DEPB) scheme were detected in which certain exporters were found exporting goods at a highly inflated value and thereby getting higher credit in their DEPB licence.

(d) Misuse of Drawback Scheme. The drawback scheme has also been found prone to misuse. There have been cases of drawback being claimed without realisation of export proceeds, misdeclaration of description of goods and over-invoicing of the value of exports with a view to obtain a higher drawback than due. Another disturbing feature is the instances of claiming drawback on fraudulent documents without export of any goods whatsoever.

(e) Misuse of 100% EOU. Cases have been detected involving diversion of goods imported duty free under the 100% Export Oriented Unit (EOU) scheme to the local market instead of using the same in production of goods for export.

(f) Misuse of EPCG Scheme. The Export Promotion Capital Goods (EPCG) scheme has been prone to misuse and a large number of cases of misuse have been detected. The violations have ranged from non-fulfilment of export obligation to outright diversion of duty free imported machinery or its sale in the market.

IV. Counterfeiting of Indian Currency

The counterfeiting is primarily done with a view to destabilise the economy of a country. The circulation of counterfeit notes in our country showed an increasing trend in the year 1998, 1999 and 2000. The counterfeiting is usually resorted to in higher denominations, since it is easier to smuggle and also it inflicts serious damage as well.

Therefore, we see the counterfeit currencies of Rs. 500 and Rs. 100 denominations. Whereas on one end these activities undermine the economy, these are also extensively used for subversive activities to threaten the national security. Although there have been substantial seizures of such currency by Mumbai Police, Mumbai Customs and also by the Punjab Police, but the fact that such counterfeit currency has been seized by various law enforcing agencies all over India gives us an indication how daunting challenge has been thrown on such agencies to curb the menace.

It is not that counterfeiting of currency notes is a new phenomenon, even during 1945-60, counterfeiting was noticed which was primarily in the notes of Rs. 1 and Rs. 10 denominations. Most probably these were the activities of certain unscrupulous gangs whose main intention was to become rich overnight and such offences could be effectively countered since there are sufficient safeguards in the Indian Penal Code. The situation is getting out of control since counterfeiting is being sponsored by a certain sovereign state and then being smuggled across to destabilised our economy.

An interrogator's job becomes more complex since he has to unearth the entire scheme of smuggling route, syndicates, organisations and intention of smuggling. The interrogator has also to have sound knowledge and skill to ascertain as to what is a counterfeit currency. This cannot be done overnight and very dedicated effort is needed to develop the skill to ascertain the same. A comparative study of the genuine and Counterfeit Note would be of immense value and this could be listed as under: -

(a) Quality and type of paper.

(b) Quality of printing.

(c) Quality of ink.

(d) Details of security features, which are copied.

(e) Types of machines used like offset printing machine or photocopy methods.

(f) Cotton content as counterfeit currency usually utilises ordinary quality paper made of wood pulp.

(g) Security thread is embedded in genuine notes at paper sheet formation.

The quantum of the counterfeit currency being smuggled in our country cannot really be quantified as sporadic seizures do not signify much since this is the easiest commodity, which can be effectively concealed and smuggled. The interrogator has to develop the skill of a seasoned printer of currency to pin down the carrier of such counterfeit currency and unearth the entire network.

V. Banking Frauds

Now let us switch over to great Bank loot appearing in media some time back as the great Indian Bank robbery of Rs. 11,00,00,00,00,000. This amount is over and above money raised by shares and debentures, which may be in the same range, if not more. Obviously such money too has also gone down the drain. The non-recovery of money borrowed by the corporate sector entrepreneurs from the public financial institutions is a very disturbing phenomenon, since they refuse to pay on the grounds that they have no capability to pay. Some approach BIFR to get declared sick and the big sharks approach the Courts to stonewall the recovery by employing the best legal talents in the country. This money was sufficient to meet our colossal defence burden for two years or open a school in every village across the country. Even the quantification of these unpaid loans may be a very conservative estimate because there is no consolidated list. There is no ambiguity that defaulters are very powerful and they will leave no stone unturned by putting pressure on lenders to go slow, besides taking advantage of the loopholes of the law. With complete disregard to pitiable conditions of thousand workers rendered jobless after lockouts, the big fish continue to live their private life with luxury. It is any one's guess that banks and financial institutions are to be blamed equally. Whenever a leading industrialist approaches for loans hundreds of crores are advanced on the basis of faulty documentation, unreal appraisal of the project with minimum of security back up. Collusion of functionaries of the lending institutions, projection of falsified health in the accounts of the borrower, political strings, etc. - are all cumulatively responsible for such financial disasters. We have not learnt much from the Securities Scam of 1992 and Late Harshad Mehta continues to head the list of individual borrowers. Coupled with the bank loans, which at best shall remain unpayable because seizures and sales of assets would not be sufficient. The sufferings of thousands of investors who purchased the shares of these companies have also to be taken into account. UTI scam of 1998 is a classic example where poor investor's money was loaned to questionable players of the equity market. In fact more than the borrower, it is the lender who is the culprit because he is treated as pious cow and there is no liability on their part. The investigations into the past scams therefore were not so fruitful to plug the loopholes to eliminate possibilities of collusion and wilful conspiracy of lenders resulting into bad loans. Failures of the lending institutions too, as they fail to draw trust deed, callous appraisal of security or initiation of timely action for recovery of investor's money. Government have taken a bold decision by passing securitisation and reconstruction of Financial Assets Enforcement of Security Interest Bill 2000 but what happens when there are no sufficient assets to commensurate with the loan recovery, one cannot expect that the Government come out with the bail out package, accountability angles, complicity and dereliction of duties on the part of lending institution have also to be examined. After all the Government cannot sit as a moot spectator when the scam is wilfully created for ulterior motives. The investigator is paranoid by the sheer magnitude and complexity of the problem, firstly, because of his own lack of expertise and influence of big players. Surprisingly there was never any banking fraud cell with most of the enforcement agencies and it was police alone which was forced to act with Indian Penal Code as a sole attacking weapon. Infrastructure expertise to investigate were rather non-existent. When the securities scam came into surface in early nineties, there used to be a joke as to how to punish Harshad Mehta and under which Act. On the face of it, there appeared to be nothing wrong; no wonder CBI was being blamed for harassment by the perpetrators of the crime.

I remember against this background there was a talk of constituting a banking fraud cell in the Central Economic Intelligence Bureau and a very senior official of the Bureau who later retired as Director of the CBI, made a very serious study. No wonder CBI is the first agency, which has the banking fraud cell. The question arises as to whether investigating officers are capable of undertaking such investigations (?), because unless and until one is familiar with mechanism of banking operations, manipulations of Chartered Accountants responsible for falsification of balance sheets of the company, the investigator is pathetically ill-equipped.

The overall view of the economic crime scenario vividly demonstrates that this is major cause of successful running of the parallel economy in our country. An interrogator faces a very tough task to develop the expertise, skill and temperament to meet the challenges not only because of the enormity of the crime but also because of the academics involved to develop the requisite know-how and expertise to outwit the offenders. Although results to meet the challenge have been quite satisfactory, it is high time to lay more emphasis on selection of the right type of personnel for the job and right type of intensive training since our conventional training to counter the economic crimes is definitely proving to be outdated.

2

Infrastructure

Talking of infrastructure of an interrogation centre may surprise many. But the absence of adequate infrastructure is bound to jeopardize smooth and fruitful outcome of any investigative effort. At times it may even adversely affect the career prospects of concerned official in the event of any untoward incidents taking place. Many custodial deaths or injuries can be avoided if we follow basic norms and suitable arrangements are made to eliminate untoward incidents by taking care of at least basic infrastructure.

We have a tendency to begin the interrogation right from the point of interception. This tendency may arise out of over enthusiasm or even lack of formal training. Distressing part is that we have even tendency to use third degree methods in complete public view. To some extent it is understandable because it takes lot of efforts for days and weeks together on the part of the intercepting team causing mental and physical fatigue resulting into restlessness. I remember one of the surveillance operation lasted for fifteen days in the month of June with day temperatures soaring to 45 degree Celsius. A notorious smuggler from Gujarat comfortably holed in Old Delhi had to go to Ahmedabad with 35 kgs. of contraband gold. The surveillance was mounted at 10 exit points leading to Ahmedabad. Further, leave alone shelter even drinking water was not easily available. We could have intercepted him at the starting point but preferred to nab him while he was on the wheels as he had thrown a challenge that since Gujarat Police could never catch him, how come the Directorate of Revenue Intelligence official could succeed. He was nabbed on the fifteenth day at

Kapashera check post as he entered the Haryana state. Now imagine the poor man's misery when about a dozen officials pounced on him and beat him black and blue in full public view. Those who did not get the chance smashed his car to release their anger. Such are but natural reactions but not in consonance with the professional training. In the melee he could have given the slip, or even public may have come to his rescue unwittingly, considering that an innocent person was being thrashed by anti-social elements. Thanks that in the year 1984, the print and electronic media were not so news hungry for spicy stories as we find them today with their teams of cameraman spread all over from snow heights of Kargil to dense forests of Satyamanglam in Tamil Nadu. It is, therefore, mandatory that the team should disappear speedily from the place of interception and take the accused to safe and secure interrogation centre - a very vital aspect of infrastructure. But what is a safe and secure place? The ideal location of the interrogation centre is the basement. If for some reasons there is no basement available the centre should be established on the first floor of the building. Although, there are many constraints owing to paucity of office accommodation but in no circumstances this requirement should be compromised. Numerous incidents have occurred where attempts by the accused to escape with a view to avoid questioning have resulted into death or fatal injuries. This not only demoralizes the interrogation team but hampers the investigation as well. It has counter productive results because the orientation of the team shifts from interrogation to damage control. Custodial deaths or serious injuries also erodes the public confidence in the process of law and we may loose the cooperation of other accused or eyewitnesses which are so vital in reconstructing the entire scenario of the crime. The entire interrogation centre should be grilled and special attention should be paid to bathrooms and toilets as these are unguarded and easy escape routes since the accused is out of view and at liberty to plan and execute the escape smoothly. Sentries should be posted in sensitive escape routes outside in plain clothes who should be armed in case the detenu is a high risk client. Sentries posted outside should carefully watch the suspicious movements of the individuals and vehicles. Persons loitering aimlessly in the vicinity or found static with no plausible reasons should be watched carefully and mental profile of such persons should be sketched in the mind carefully. Accomplices engaged in execution of the escape usually position themselves in bus stop, tea stalls, cigarette vendor's shop where they can while away hours without being noticed. Unattended vehicles with tinted glasses and scooters and motorcycles in the area should be watched and their registration number noted down. It has been experienced that usually motor cycles and scooters are used as a getaway vehicle at least in the initial stages because of obvious advantage as they can conveniently jump the traffic signals, enter into bye-lanes and also sail through congested traffic jams. To foil such attempts suitable persons with adequate strength and vehicles should be earmarked and they should be able to react swiftly. Although all police vehicles are fitted with wireless but in case the investigation agency is from some other department like Customs, Narcotics Control Bureau, Foreign Exchange Enforcement Directorate they should be fitted with the wireless having inter-connectivity with the Police Control Room because they have much wider presence and can react more swiftly and effectively. We should never forget that gangsters have carried out successful rescue operations in busy court rooms and even in Police Stations to take out their comrade from distress.

Few years back while I was undergoing a training course with a high profile agency we were told that interrogation room should be sparsely furnished. I could not fathom the rationale behind it and therefore could not co-relate as to in which way it would be advantageous to the interrogators. Then at the spur of the moment I recalled an incident and realized its import. Way back in July, 1967, as an young officer in the Army, I was made the leader of a fighting patrol and was directed to proceed to LUTIN Pass on Mc-Mohan Line in Kameng frontier division in the North Eastern Frontier Agency, which is now called Arunachal Pradesh. The pass was five days walking distance, located at a height of 18239 ft. above from the sea level and was only accessible during the month of July in a year. I was also directed to stay put at the Pass for forty eight hours and look around for Chinese infiltrators and react as the situation may demand. It was a very strong patrol comprising of thirty selected tough and sharp shooter infantry soldiers. We dispensed with part of our authorized ration entitlement and substituted it with live ammunition to reduce weight on our back. Every one was really filled with tremendous enthusiasm. We reached the pass but what we felt was an experience out of this world. The mother earth was awe-inspiring beautiful as you could gaze hundred of square kilometers of un-inhabited empty mountains in the Chinese territory. It was frightening too, a strange feeling that we are in the moon and would never be able to return to earth - an unreal feeling of helplessness. Emptiness creates an impression of vacuum which in turn arouses anxiety; uncertainty and fear.

Sparsely furnished interrogation room generates strange feeling of uncertainty, the space however limited replicates the vacuum, a strong feeling of nothingness. It not only blunts the thinking but also creates a fear which cannot be comprehended and the accused gets totally disoriented and out of focus. We should therefore have minimum of furniture absolutely necessary to conduct the serious business.

There cannot be a more pathetic sight if any interrogator resorting to writing from the word go, the accused enters the interrogation chamber. It helps the accused in gaining his composure and creates an impression in the mind of the accused that the interrogator is ill-prepared to do the job and therefore updates his defence mechanism to de-rail the investigation. Hence the necessity of recording devices.

These are very essential aids and cannot be dispensed with. But these should be in-built and so placed so as to be invisible to naked and probing eyes and the accused should never be able to gather the impression that his conversation is being recorded or he is being video filmed. In this context I would like to share an experience. Way back in 1989, a UK based gang of robbers, all NRIs, targeted one Russian businessman, to rob him of Rs.14 crores in India when he took out that money from his account on his visit to India. They came to India studied the situation and found that robbery was not possible owing to effective presence of Delhi Police. They went back to UK, posed as informers with the officials of our High Commission in London and volunteered to become Hawala operators with an intention to lure the Russian businessman to give them the money for transfer to some tax haven island by Hawala. They were directed to Central Economic Intelligence Bureau of India for necessary follow-up action. It was very strange to volunteer as Hawala operator in unknown distant land as there is no dearth of efficient Hawala operators in Chandni Chowk who play with hundreds of crores in siphoning off the Indian currency through non-banking channels. They stayed in a luxury five star hotel for a fortnight and their life-style evoked further curiosity. It was therefore decided to interrogate them thoroughly and their entire conversation was video-recorded. They themselves admitted that they wanted to commit robbery and finding it not feasible they settled down for reward money of two crores and discomforts of jail for one year under preventive detention in Tihar Jail as we were bound to catch them as well. Considering that they were too dangerous informers and could take us for a ride by misleading us, Central Bureau of Investigation was also roped in and the then Director of the CBI, who was my superior officer in the CEIB, was too pleased to give me a detachment of commandos to deal with the unforeseen contingencies. Unfortunately for some unknown reasons the gang fell apart and their plan could not be translated on the ground, although the deposit of 12 crores was later seized under the Income Tax Act without associating the informers. This incident clearly brings out the importance of recording devices in the interrogation centre and is certainly of tremendous advantage.

The interrogation center should be isolated from rest of the office and away from curious eyes and not located in a thoroughfare. No boards, signposts should be ever displayed so as to give any indication as to for which purpose the place has been designated. To safeguard against the security of the place, such places could be codenamed 'Meditation Center' or 'Yoga Center'. One can always employ his poetic inclinations to give such place a code name without revealing the identity or purpose of the centre.

Yet another requirement of the interrogation centre but equally important is that it should be sound proof. Invariably our offices are located in busy and populated areas where there is heavy traffic of vehicles and noise pollution causes not of distraction. Further, there may be number of accused outside and they should never be able to overhear as to on what lines the interrogation is proceeding, as it would enable them to build up effective and evasive mechanism to mislead our investigations. The room should have effective and suitable lighting arrangements as even imaginative light fittings can be used to break the resistance of the accused. Sanctity of the interrogation centre is of utmost importance and entry to the centre should be restricted and except for those who are really concerned with the task, none should be allowed to gain entry.

And finally, to save the botheration of knocking at the twenty four hour open chemist shop in the city, keep the centre equipped with the first aid box containing requisite medicines. However, this is not to imply that any one would really need it. Of course, as to what medicines the first aid kit should comprise of one will have to learn by his own experience.

3

Curtain Rises

Interrogation is most neglected area of our investigative endeavors. It is usually treated as a ritual as we get lax after a substantive seizure has been made or a prized catch has fallen into our net. We tend to forget that the man in the custody has to be co-related with the offence and irrefutable evidence has to be brought on record which can withstand the scrutiny of the court. Usually a junior functionary or some one found not doing anything is told to record the submissions by the accused. Obviously such efforts can only bring incorrect facts which fall flat at the time of cross-examination in a court of law. In addition to render the respondent's lawyer defenceless one should also be prepared to answer judicious querries of the Hon'ble Court. This can best be achieved when the task assigned is taken in the right earnest.

Constitution of the interrogation team is therefore of a paramount importance. At the apex level there is bound to be head of the investigative branch who may not necessarily associate with the entire process of interrogation but the entire evidence should pass through his scanner so that valuable guidance is available to us at the right moment. Usually we feel shy of bringing the facts of interrogation to our superiors primarily with a view to ensure that our own incompetence is not exposed. This is a very negative attitude as besides harming the cause of investigation we also deny an opportunity to learn from the experience of our seniors.

Just under the head of investigation team, the interrogation team should consist of two components, i.e.,

(A) Peripheral team

We should induct officers in this team who have flair for interrogation but are in the process of learning the tricks of the trade. Most of us learn while on the job and in due course this team will graduate to take up more serious responsibilities. In doing so we shall also build up a strong force of reserve officers to handle number of cases simultaneously. Officers inducted in this team should be suitably briefed sufficiently in advance so that no aspect is lost sight off. They should also have exposure so that other law enforcing agencies can be associated. To illustrate the point let us take the example of claiming duty drawback and defrauding the national exchequer by resorting to forgery. Such an act or omission would simultaneously contravene the provisions of the Indian Penal Code and Police also is competent to initiate criminal proceedings under the relevant Act. Proceedings under the Customs Act derive authority from Code of Criminal Procedure and if one does not have working knowledge of the relevant sections it will be a total disaster; knowledge of language, culture, customs and traditions of the land of the accused will be of tremendous advantage and should scrupulously brought on record since it will be of great help to analyze the mind of the accused when the core team steps in to take the baton forward. Above all, in the peripheral team there should always be one or two talkative persons with ready wit, who can talk for hours to confuse the accused without revealing their mind. I remember one incident about the usefulness of such talkative officer who could bore any one to death by his irrelevant talk and out of sheer frustration you could divulge the information he needed. We had to search the residential premises of one smuggler in Delhi and while identifying the place to be searched we realized that this could not be the place of an operator dealing in lucrative illegal activity having network in Singapore and Hong Kong. So the talkative man of the team came to our rescue and offered his services to get the details of exact premises provided he was not taken in the search operation and wanted a lady officer to accompany him. His request was conceded and he went inside. We were getting desperate as to why he did not come out for long. We do not know what transpired inside but we were informed by the lady officer that he was enjoying the hot cup of tea. By masquerading as a wealthy businessman from Ludhiana city where he had never been, he build up a very convincing story and got the full information from the inmates of the house. The areas which the peripheral team should stress upon are :-

(a) Personal data:

((i) Date of birth

ii) Place of birth

(iii) Education and details of the institutes where educated.

(iv) Composition of the family and their status and activities.

(b) Relatives, friends and acquaintances their residential addresses, telephone numbers, their activities.

(c) Professional background:

(i) History of employment

(ii) Reasons of shifting the jobs

(iii) Salaries drawn.

(d) Financial status:

(i) Details of the property both moveable and immovable acquired and held in own name or benami.

(ii) Properties inherited

(iii) Details of properties held by relatives, friends and acquaintances including benami properties of such persons.

(e) Religious beliefs and political affiliations including affiliations with religious groups including certain organisations if any as there are numerous front

made the head master of a school in Pakistan occupied Kashmir for salary purposes. He was therefore rightly picked up by us for interrogation. Call it my inexperience since I had only three years service or my enthusiasm for quick results which I wanted to show to my Brigade Commander on his arrival the following day who was away from the Headquarters, I failed to get him examined medically before the questioning started. To our bad luck, he collapsed by midnight and his vital signs of life were found to be missing. We immediately shifted him to a field hospital where he was put on life support systems. Luckily he survived. Although Tithwal valley was not so volatile in early seventies nevertheless there was a huge demonstration but they withdrew quietly as they realized that it was more because of his body ailments and he was being taken care of. But more was to follow. The Brigadier was summoned by the Chief Minister and given a nasty bit of his mind. Furious as he was on his arrival, my seniors ordered that I should receive him, an unusual thing as a Brigade Intelligence Officer was a too junior functionary. Mountains are very notorious for cloud burst and hell broke out upon me. My Brigadier although a graduate of famous Government college of Lahore as he studied there before partition, had a unique distinction of employing three language formula while dressing down an officer. So the choicest abuses in English, Hindi and Punjabi were hurled at me which I accepted sportingly with a grim face. All of a sudden he became very volatile and said “you bastard, what would you have done had he died” and without pausing further said, “both of us would have been in jail by now”. Helpless although I was nevertheless my patience was running out after having come under heavy volume of fire. Mustering courage in a stubborn voice, I too shot back “Very simple, I would have thrown him in Krishna Ganga river to be fished out by the Pakistani Army authorities in Muzaffarabad”. Although, I could never have done that but he appreciated my confidence, patted me on my back and said he liked bold and courageous officers -

"Get lost from my sight and have a large Rum on my account" although he was a teetotaler. To the surprise of my senior colleagues, I came out unscathed smiling. This very Brigadier later walked into Dhaka in Bangladesh operation and was instrumental in disarming General Niazi, the Pakistani Corps Commander in East Pakistan now called Bangladesh. My client also after being discharged from the Hospital walked into POK and resumed charge of the school in Pakistan occupied Kashmir. I was later told by the medical authorities that he was a chronic diabetic and heart patient and could not bear the shock of interrogation. The moral of the whole incident is as to how small slips can cost dearly as we failed to elicit any information from him which could have been of immense value to our security forces and most importantly we could neither lay hands on other members of the gang nor we could unearth the modus operandi to devise counter intelligence methodology.

of the informer and he was brought to office. The IB officials were aghast with surprise when they saw that the informer was being given third degree treatment and within an hour he broke down completely and the true story was revealed as under.

The informer was young postgraduate Muslim gentleman from Calcutta and was employed as Telex Operator by the garment exporter. By virtue of his high academic qualifications and pleasing manners he became the most trusted man of the proprietor and virtually ran the entire business. He was given the keys of the office premises and thus was the first man to come and the last man to leave the office. Unfortunately, he fell in love with a young unmarried girl employed in the office and his advances were not taken kindly by the exporter and he was rebuked a number of times. He therefore decided to teach his employer a lesson and while everybody left the office he stayed late and passed on messages which he drafted himself to some one in the name and address of a serving Pakistani Intelligence Chief. Admittedly we were totally biased against the garment exporter and consequences of any wrong inferences would have been disastrous for his social prestige, business activities and career prospects of his relatives who were still serving in the Army. After all every time our sixth sense cannot rescue us from the wrong track. Free from bias attitude should not be construed that the fellow is totally innocent. It only connotes that more hard work and patience is the requirement of the hour and we should be more than willing to slog.

Interrogation can really become a cake walk if rapport is established between interrogator and the accused. But one should not get misguided by the dictionary meaning of rapport. It does not mean that every one should throw caution to the wind and become friendly and start hobnobbing with the person to be interrogated. To that extent the word is misnomer. It connotes we conduct in manner that the accused gets a false sense of security which he tends to believe that it is true and gets totally uninhibited and starts co-operating. Care should be taken that not each one of the team should establish the rapport. Suffice to say that if one interrogator succeeds to touch the emotional cord of the accused that is likely to yield positive results, the rest of the interrogators should continue to have stiff neck and maintain serious posture to create uncertainty in the mind of the accused. How it can be achieved is the moot question and cannot be easily answered. Every situation will require a fresh careful approach and handling. We were interrogating a very high profile economic offender enjoying clout with top ranking politicians and bureaucrats which he had developed as a Captain in Air India before switching over to garment export business. Even in response to simple questions he threw tantrums, threatened officials creating impression that we were wasting our time. In fact the whole team was overawed. After the peripheral team had done the job I appeared in the scene. Since he was much senior to me in age, the first thing I asked him whether with his permission I could smoke a cigarette. It immediately had a desired effect and he profusely appreciated the gesture by getting up. I informed him that he was a senior citizen, a very responsible member of the society and deserved all the respect from us. During the course of interrogation, he became very spontaneous and forthright, abusing even his bureaucratic contacts who gave him false confidence which motivated him to defraud the government. Needless to say his voluntary confessions landed him in judicial custody for few weeks.

I also recall yet another encounter which is rather more amusing. We rounded up a member of a syndicate who had specialized in smuggling of high value consumer goods in trade quantities. They had fixed set of officers with whom they synchronized their landing at Delhi Airport while coming with the contraband goods from Hong Kong and Singapore and always walked through the green channel. Unfortunately, the syndicate leader was very meticulous in

Barring certain exceptions every offender develops a tremendous willpower to overcome the ordeal and tries to hoodwink the interrogator. He is constantly aware of the fact that a day will come when his game will be up. It is because of such consciousness, he conditions his mind in such a manner that he develops a strong willpower to resist the interrogation and we call such persons die hard criminals. Even such persons will ultimately not escape the consequences of their illegal actions in the wake of sustained interrogation which I will demonstrate in the succeeding paras.

The escape route of a die-hard criminal lies between memory and story he puts forth. Every criminal has exceptionally good memory around which he weaves a story. If memory is hampered, the story is bound to become incoherent and unconvincing. Thus the capacity of the story telling has to be incapacitated to reach at the bottom of truth. This can be achieved by numerous ways. Rapid and probing questions can severely impair his memory. I was sent to Amritsar from Delhi to interrogate an individual although he was not at all involved in the smuggling activities but instrumental in laundering the ill-gotten money by converting it into real estate of agricultural land, flats and shops. The gentleman was an elderly person in his early eighties, semi-illiterate as he could hardly write except Punjabi in Gurumukhi script. I was very surprised when I found him giving long pauses while answering very simple questions. I asked him as to why he was taking so much time to answer such simple and innocent questions and I learnt a very important lesson of my career when he candidly replied that he was not bothered by such simple questions but he had to take care of the questions which would arise out of his answers. Therein lies the importance of rapid questioning. If we give time to the accused to replenish his armoury of memory, a misleading answer will be forthcoming to derail the process of interrogation. Similarly, it is not the time for exchanging pleasantries now or of asking irrelevant questions but the right time to shoot the probing questions to shatter his confidence and will power to elicit a factually true reply. Probing questions create the impression in the mind of the subject being interrogated that we are aware of all his misdeeds and recording of evidence is a mere formality and his will power to resist gets a severe blow. A barrage of questions does not necessarily imply that a factually true reply is ensured. Far from true. Totally false and misleading answers are bound to be given and therefore after gap of some times these questions have to be repeated at a number of times. This is done with a view to take advantage of his failing memory. Constant pounding by questions is bound to have telling effect on his memory and he is bound to succumb to pressure and give up the resistance. In case it is noticed that no headway is being made, questions can be formulated by misquoting the answers given in the past to create confusion. Confusion effectively punctures the air filled balloon of memory and can effectively be employed to break the willpower of the accused. Whenever such misquoting is resorted to, care should be taken to ensure that the answer is not fresh in his memory. If the suspect gets an impression that you are misquoting him he may get an inkling that you have exhausted yourself and there is nothing with you to pin him down and in turn it may boost his sagging morale. It is therefore imperative that misquoting is resorted to only when certain time has lapsed and the subject is showing visible signs of fatigue and resignation. At every stage of questioning the accused has to be ridiculed, embarrassed and humiliated. One can always create an impression that print and electronic media is waiting outside in strength to cover the story and media coverage of the event is bound to bring disgrace to his family, relatives and acquaintances and to escape such disgrace, it is in his own interest to come to the point and save his kith and kin from humiliation. Offenders engaged in espionage activities are very sensitive to ridicule and humiliation as the stigma sticks on them for life time and their will power to resist is considerably weakened.

In fact when they are without drug for a considerable time they are very depressed, incoherent and not at all co-operative notwithstanding their thinking faculty is totally impaired. You do not have to extend any hospitality to them as they themselves would ask for it and to ensure they get their usual daily quota of narcotic drugs and with a view to ensure its assured supply, they come out with very authentic and credible statements implicating themselves. They are very candid once they have consumed their daily quota and make a honest and true voluntarily statement when their mental facilities are at best. One cannot get anything from them when they are undergoing withdrawal symptoms. Hence the criteria of hospitality has to be decided as to what would be conducive to elicit voluntarily and factually correct statement.

The question may arise as to from where the psychotropic substance can be procured. It is a well established fact that in illicit drug trade except for the key syndicate leaders, others are addicts. In fact before they are recruited and inducted in the network the drug cartel ensures that their carriers become addict to ensure they are totally dependent and on mercy of their employers. We do not have to bother as the addict would invariably carry the dose on person for such contingency and what he will ask for is the permission to take the dose and why we should have problem if it helps our cause.

Feigning criminals can also be used to illicit information. Two criminals get friendly very fast and if the die-hard criminal get an impression that other has spilled the beans the will power of the subject get a severe blow and in the course of sustained interrogation the criminal is bound to call it a day. When a large number of members of syndicate are rounded up, there are always certain weak links in the chain. Sometimes they come with a very unusual request that they be given third degree treatment in lieu of their voluntary and true statement. It is really amazing but it is true. In fact they are mortally scarred of the 'Boss' as the syndicate leader is addressed to with respect in the underworld and they want to have bodily evidence of torture to mislead and win the sympathy and also save themselves from reprisal of the boss. A stage managed fake show can be created of giving such treatment as it would demoralize the syndicate leader. It is noticed that the 'Boss' would never like to undergo such treatment in the presence of his gang as the myth of his superiority would be demolished and therefore he would come forward tamely to narrate the real story.

With the globalization of crime it is likely that an interrogator may come across a subject with whom he just cannot communicate owing to language barrier, the job thus becomes difficult. When you talk to your subject directly body language conveys the right signals to the interrogator and once an interpreter is inducted he gets assured. There is lot of time gap by the time question reaches him and he gets mentally prepared to frame his reply. The selection of the interpreter is a tricky job because the interpreter and the interrogator have to be on the same wave length in relation to background of the case, material available on the accused and what is intended to be achieved. Thus, an interpreter is virtually a duplicate of the interrogation team since he alone can effectively pose the questions. The interpreter should also be of unimpeachable integrity and of very high moral character who is above temptations and not guided by any ulterior considerations. I have been very fortunate to have interpreters of this class. An Uzbek seaman (erstwhile USSR) was intercepted with contraband gold valued at over 3.2 crores. Since we could not communicate with him we availed the services of an interpreter who happened to be a young lady in her thirties. She was an MA and Ph.D. in Russian language from Moscow University. Contrary to the usual belief, standard Russian language was never spoken in all confederating states of the erstwhile USSR. Identical is scenario in India as well. A professor of Hindi language / literature will not be altogether comfortable when confronted with dialects of Hindi as spoken in Bihar, Rajasthan or Haryana. Every dialect has its own nuances and requires skill and experience to interpret it. Fortunately as this interpreter had acquired degree as a resident student in Moscow, she was quiet familiar with various dialects as well. Once she was briefed thoroughly about her role, she never waited for questions to be framed by us. She would frame the question herself and would not rest will she got the correct reply and would go on grilling the accused by her persistent questioning. She got so engrossed in her role with such dedication that at times she would literally become violent and we would have to restrain her from loosing temper. She did an excellent job and when it came to remuneration she declined and requested that a certificate only be given to her appreciating her role as an interpreter. During the trial of the case in a Mumbai court, she was cross-examined for three days by the defense lawyer but she stood her ground. It is matter of great solace that even the Magistrate lauded her performance in the open court. These are however exception. Nevertheless with little careful planning such interpreters can be found and can be used effectively to overcome the mental blockage between an interrogator and the subject.

We have spoken about recording devices in our infrastructure chapter. It is worthwhile to have voice samples of such criminals in our record. The voice samples always retain the general linguistic and phonetic features of some one's spoken language and remain more or less constant throughout one's life and can be of immense evidential value whenever voice sample tests are needed at a later part of time in some case. In fact it should be a ritual in highly sensitive cases since crime becomes way of life of criminals who chose such career and are bound to figure in some other crime at a later date as well. I remember an encounter with a smuggler who had a posh residential Kothi in Greater Kailash in Delhi and had a lucrative business in trading of watches in Lajpat Rai Market. Somehow I had some role to play in sending him to Tihar Jail for preventive detention in smuggling cases, a number of times. When I posed him the question when he was walking in third time that he should give up smuggling he asked me the counter question as to where I would search if I lost my purse in Chandni Chowk? In Karol Bagh or Chandni Chowk? My natural reply was that I will definitely search it in Chandni Chowk. Prompt came the counter-reply that he was doing the same as the smuggling was the only way to replenish his losses suffered after seizure of his smuggled watches and payment of hefty fees to his advocates in court cases in the past which in any case would linger on for years. In a way he may be right but the fact remains that such nefarious activities become their established business and sometimes passes on even to succeeding generations.

The biggest handicap which we face in undertaking an interrogation is the time constraint. The moment an accused comes in our custody we have to produce him before the Magistrate within 24 hours for a police remand or judicial remand. Now the moot questions arises whether within such short period, is it humanly possible to crack a complex case. It is an ostrich like approach where we do not appreciate the ground realities and the accused gets benefit of the statutory limitations imposed on an interrogator. After all when such restrictions were imposed the nature of crime was simple and easy to handle. The complexity of crime has gone sea-change, human right activists, best legal brains come to rescue of the accused. Just imagine if one of the accused of fidayeen gang who attacked our Parliament on 13th December 2001 was caught alive could any one have solved the case within twenty-four hours. Even Americans have realized the absurdities imposed on them and consequent upon attack on World Trade Centre have dispensed with the concept of fundamental rights as security has become their main concern. Al Qaeda detenues of over 36 countries of the world detained by the USA in Guantanamo Bay (in Cuba) and subjected to intensive interrogation virtually in subhuman conditions is a point which we have to ponder seriously to consider amending the laws specially in relation to offences against sovereignty of states in general and against humanity in particular. Notwithstanding such limitation we should not be in a hurry while interrogating an accused involved in prejudicial activities injurious to integrity of a nation. Let us appreciate that enormous destruction and loss of life in World Trade Centre would not have been possible without well-oiled infrastructure and financial support as the investigations have revealed so far. Thus, terrorist activities and economic offences are two sides of the same coin. In fact, without the connivance of the economic offenders Osama-Bin-Laden could never have succeeded. Back home in Kashmir valley same is the scenario. Drug money has been pumped in to recruit foreign mercenaries who kill innocent with glee and impunity.

Against this background it is imperative that we do not jettison the basic tenets and fundamental principles of interrogation and come what may, you should be never in hurry. The moot question is how to overcome the statutory limit of twenty hours before the Magistrate without circumventing the law. It is seen that after an accused has been remanded to Police or Judicial custody he tends to become non-cooperative and even hostile, since he gets sufficiently tutored by his lawyers, friends and relatives. He overcomes the initial shock and in due course gets composed and even wise as to how to thwart the process of law. It may not apply to high profile criminals caught for heinous crimes espionage or terrorist activities but persons engaged in economic offences are soft targets since they have family, business concerns moveable and immovable property. To abscond would jeopardize their social status and would also cripple their licit or illicit economic activities and therefore they prefer to co-operate. Such persons can be allowed to go and summoned again to tender their statement. They should be kept under discreet surveillance. In the event of their co-operation not forthcoming, there are sufficient judicial remedies available to coerce them into joining the investigation. Independent cases as provided in the criminal procedure code can be filed, they can be got declared as proclaimed offenders and their property attached. If we adopt this line of investigation then two points should be always kept in mind. Firstly, no probing questions should be asked in the initial stages and thrust should be on collecting as much information as possible, which are relevant to the case. Secondly, discreet static or mobile surveillance should be always be mounted to keep watch over the movements and activities till his next appearance. These are painstaking efforts but pay rich dividends as we gather first hand information about the accused which can be basis of subsequent interrogation. If prima-facie indications come to surface meriting arrest, the probing questions should be on the day when the accused is likely to be arrested.

During the period he is away and next appearance, the accused may and shall think out certain stories to wriggle him out. Do not believe such chicken feed stories and discard them and start all over again. Tire out the accused and drain his memory to the extent that he is left with no will-power to create any more stories.

In case of criminals suspected to be engaged in more serious offences like nexus with terrorists, espionage syndicates etc., a more careful approach is needed. We should insist on custodial interrogation and pray for Police remand, by and large the courts are very appreciative of such essentiality and do not hesitate to order Police remand. This shall however depend how skillfully the Remand Application has been drafted. In our over-enthusiasm to impress the court, numerous facts are incorporated primarily based on assumptions, which create an impression that the investigations are more or less over and Police remand may not be justifiable. The necessity of such remand should be brought on record by elucidating the gravity of the offences and bringing out very clearly as to how refusal of Police remand would adversely affect the public interest.

There are various precautions which we should take during the course of interrogation and violation thereof should be treated as strict taboo. A good effort may become inconsequential thus rendering the whole exercise futile.

Never indulge in loose talks before the subject. It is noticed that to release our own frustrations when things are not falling in its place, we resort to such tendencies. There should be firm impression in the mind of the suspect that we are in the midst of a serious business and its gravity should be ingrained in the mind of the accused. Any loose talk would give a breather to suspect to gain composure and confidence which will be contrary to our intended aim and objective. Loose talks would be instrumental in soothing the nerves of the accused and therefore the atmosphere should be strictly formal creating awe, uncertainty and fear in the mind of the subject.

Never make a promise not even a false promise. It is because of the fact that the accused is not alone in the conspiracy of an act and a promise would create a situation where he will successfully sell out a false story and you would tend to believe it to be true under the presumption that since disclosures have been made after a promise and therefore must be true. In fact promises induce false belief in the mind of the interrogator which is totally divorced from reality.

No statement should be concluded before the subject. It sends a wrong signal that questioning is over and the interrogator has nothing more to ask. In fact, we should have brain storming sessions with our seniors separately to find out as to what points needs to be probed further and also tie-up the loose ends. We should always create an impression in the mind of the subject that he has landed in a dark tunnel which has no end. Such impression will go long way in creating confusion, uncertainty and fear which will give us avenues to explore him further.

Never allow the subject to be left unattended. He should be guarded by providing adequate guards depending upon the physic and personal traits of the accused to ensure that he does not escape. To that extent careful watch should be kept when allowed to visit toilet, etc. In any office we have always certain objects required for routine office work like blades, knife, scissors, match boxes and the like which can be dangerous if some one wants to harm himself with an intent to implicate you in a false case of causing grievous injury. These objects should always be kept outside reach and sight of the suspect to avoid unpleasant situations. In any case if an attempt is being made he should be overpowered and restrained to commit such an act. A small cut in the blood vessel can result into serious problem and in case a suspect succeeds in such attempt, prompt medical care should be provided and one should not hesitate to even file a First Information Report with the jurisdictional police to ensure a false case is not slapped on you.

We have seen a very disturbing tendency on the part of the middle level officers to issue summons and then go to sleep at their residence leaving the interrogation to the junior level officers. Professionally such behavior is highly unethical. If a summon is issued under the seal and signature of a particular officer, he should stay through out during the course of interrogation. Such officers by their sheer negligence bring embarrassment to the Department during the course of cross-examination when the prosecution is launched, since they are not privy to the developments during their absence. During absence of such officer, the junior level officer who owing to their professional immaturity or uncalled for enthusiasm create really unimaginable situations. I recall an incident where consequent upon ostensibly a custodial death of an accused certain officers were sent to his residence in wee hours to fetch an ironed kurta pajama so that he could be taken to hospital for treatment. The wife of the accused got suspicious and wrote a simple postcard to the Chief Justice of India for intervention to locate her husband. This plain and simple postcard was deemed to be a habeas corpuses petition by the Apex Court and what followed thereafter was nightmare to the concerned officers but also caused acute embarrassment to the Department. Lest we create identical situations, we have to rise beyond the call of duty to ensure that we do not bring shame to the Department.

5

Modern Technical Aids in Interrogation

The rapid advancements in the field of science and technology as well as in medicinal field have opened numerous avenues in the field of investigation. Such facilities were not available in yesteryears and an interrogator had to depend upon the brute methodology, which was not only inhuman, but at times also proved to be counter-productive. We routinely witness scenes of such techniques invariably in most of the films involving criminals. It is only partially true and probably being resorted to by investigators and only manifest frustrations of the investigative effort. Moreover third degree methods only make an accused immune to such physical torture and thus an accused develops a defence mechanism to frustrate the investigation. In fact, it only cements the offender's resolve to go into the shell and become non-communicative. Such scenario is indeed counter productive for the interrogation. Our efforts should therefore be to encourage talking howsoever irrelevant it may be. A talkative criminal is more vulnerable to questioning than the one who maintains stoic silence.

Certain human rights activists have often condemned the employment of modern investigative aids as cruelty to the subject and infringements of his fundamental rights. Such pro-active groups however fail to appreciate the fundamental rights of innocent humans who die in terrorist activities every day in various parts of the country. No human rights petition was ever filed by such groups when the insurgency was at its peak in Punjab and once the normalcy was restored there was spate of these petitions. Such trends make the intentions of these activists suspect to our common sense. Yet another valid questions which needs to be answered is the efficacy of these aids. Let us for example take the case of Lie Detector. There is total misconception in the minds of a common man and the interrogator is no exception that Lie Detector is like ATM facility of a Bank and you insert the card and get the money. Far from true, as we shall see in the succeeding paras. Similar is the case in respect of certain chemical aids which could be used in our investigative efforts undoubtedly they lead us to vital clues to persue and nothing beyond that. To that extent these are very useful tools and should be effectively employed by an interrogator to get in to the right track than getting lost in the labyrinth of wrong tracks of a complex crime.

The Lie Detector consists of three parts:-

(a) **Prenograph** - Once a subject is made to undergo the test, it records the respiratory changes taking place in the accused.

(b) **Cardio Phymograph** - It record the blood pressure and pulse rate of the person undergoing the test.

(c) **Psycho-galvano graph** - It records the skin resistance of the person when subjected to the detector test.

From the functions of the various parts of the lie detector one can draw an inference that there are broad parameters of functioning of the human body with permissible variations which are not of varying degree in any human being. Once subjected to the test such body reactions undergo a vast change which give a categorical indication that the person is not telling the truth. In essence it is the mind of the accused which is revealed through various bodily reactions which are recorded in the graph. Question also arises whether the detector has the capability to produce the desired results with equal fidelity in case a criminal is seasoned, highly motivated and has conditioned his mind sufficiently in advance to negotiate the ordeal. My own perception after having undergone a lie detector test in a training session is that the lie detector may not be of much help. Unlike DNA test or finger print matching, it is not all that a exact science and only reveals a probability. Although, it is a fact that it is only an exception and in most of the cases an individual may not be able to overcome the psychological impact of undergoing the test and may get easily exposed and will not be in a position to conceal his reactions.

It is pertinent to note that the mode of questioning remains the same as we follow in routine interrogation, exception that we may devise a well-conceived capsule of questions in advance before subjecting someone to undergo the test to obviate the possibility of being misled by a tough and shrewd mind.

In addition to lie detector, we also know yet another machine called Psychological Stress Evaluation (PSE) which records the stress on the vocal chord. The voice undergoes vital changes in a given situation like when someone is weeping, crying or laughing which give enough indication as to the credibility of the suspect while under going the test. This is currently being used by the CIA in the United States of America as a major aid in interrogation techniques. We are not aware whether this equipment has been inducted in India.

Notwithstanding the utility of these technological aids there is no denying the fact that these have certain limitations and it is the human skill and experience which only can unearth the mysteries of complex planning and execution of a crime. It is rather an indispensable tool and our emphasis should be more on training and developing the right skill to meet the challenge.

Certain chemical aids can also be used as an important aid in the armory of an interrogator. These too have been termed unethical as it tantamount to exploitation of an individual's mind at the moments of helplessness, while recovering from the after effects of the drugs administered during the interrogation. Awarding a level playing field to a criminal, as the human right activists expect, desire and insist upon, does not seem to be rational as it will seal the outcome of any vital investigations which may have potentials of serious ramifications on national security. There is equally important aspect of the issue which also cannot be lost sight of. One thing is abundantly clear that use of these aids only help the accused since the human error, bias and prejudices of the interrogator get eliminated altogether and possibility of an innocent person getting implicated is ruled out. In a lie detector test there is a possibility that a tough criminal may dodge the machine and also a weakling may show manifestations which are totally divorced from the reality. Employment of chemical aid, however eliminates altogether the bias factor and also an accused is not in a position to hoodwink the interrogator. It is however necessary that such methods should be resorted to under strict medical supervision and should not be left to those who are not aware of the side effects of such drugs. A possibility may also arise that body of the accused may not respond favorably which may cause irreparable damage to our efforts. Further, the possibility of the subject getting violent at this stage cannot be ruled out. In all these situations, the suspect has to be under constant medical supervision. A newspaper report in a national daily only few years back is an eye opener. A patient was to be operated for cataract and local anesthesia was being administered. Since the patient got violent and refused to take the local anesthesia, general anesthesia was administered which resulted in cardiac arrest and the patient could never recover from it. Ultimately a valuable life was lost and it happened in a very reputed hospital of Mumbai. Employment of such aid is therefore fraught with dangers and a very careful thought should be given before being resorted to.

There are numerous sedatives which have no side effects if given in permissible limits. These induce sleep in the suspect and if sleep is denied the suspect is bound to become incoherent, impatient and may ultimate buy sleep by telling the truth. There are certain truth serums like Sodium Pentathol, Amytal and Evipan which are equally effective. These are basically mind altering drugs, not that these demotivate a criminal completely, but for a while the motivation level evaporates and an accused is not conscious as to what he is revealing. Sodium Pentathol has been extensively used by the Federal Bureau of Investigation in Guatanamo Bay (in Cuba) on Al Qaeda members.

I may be allowed to recall an incident in response to the protagonists who oppose the use of these modern technical aids including those from the medicinal field. In fact they may be compelled to jettison their baseless perceptions altogether. While serving in the army as a Brigade Intelligence Officer, a young local boy in early thirties was intercepted by our forward troops while working in his fields and had inadvertently crossed over the Line of Control. In those days of early seventies, there were only small stone pillars to indicate the border and these incidents were of routine nature. Since a very influential local and very reliable contractor of Army gave the information about his alleged espionage activities, it was acted upon by the forward troops. Unfortunately a sheet containing full details of our deployment, strength of troops in each post and weaponry were recovered from this person. Naturally, he was handed over to the Brigade Headquarters for interrogation. The recovery of the incriminating documents was sufficient to prove his culpability. I was rather very cautious and did not want to take a risk resulting into suffering of an innocent person and his family.

We had a Mobile Field Hospital adjacent to our Brigade Headquarters Commanded by a Surgeon Lt. Colonel. He was a doctor of a different breed - a rare one at that, having earned Military Cross in 2nd world War, a gallantry award reserved for soldiers for supreme sacrifice. While commanding a medical platoon somewhere in Europe he was attached to allied troops who ran away in the face of a fierce German attack. He preferred to die with honour and against all ethics of medical profession, attacked the German post with his ill-trained, ill-equipped nursing soldiers. The irony of the fate unfolded in his favors. The Germans thought they were counter attacked by a very strong force and therefore fled away leaving their weapons and ammunitions and thus the young doctor was decorated with the Military Cross. For no reason or rhyme, he used to be present during our interrogation sessions and appreciating my dilemma offered his expert medical experience duly apologizing that his offer was against the medical ethics.

The accused was taken to operation theatre and administered general anesthesia. In fact if Ketamine is administered as general anesthesia, the results are more encouraging since the suspect goes into trance and gets totally disoriented and is available for interrogation for a longer duration. Before he could recover the doctor started slapping the suspect and started asking questions about the case. He said he was innocent and was framed by one Mohammad Shafi of New Gabra village, who was an Army Contractor and he will never forgive him. We really got the answers. I was later told by the Colonel that there is a period of two to three minutes between unconsciousness and recovery which is some thing like twilight during which the person is most uninhibited and speaks nothing but truth. In normal circumstances he could have never opened his mouth against the influential person who had access to Brigadiers and Generals by virtue of being very reliable contractor.

The emphasis shifted to interrogation of Mohammad Shafi. The facts revealed were not only amusing but alarming too. Kashmiri girls are by and large uniformly beautiful and the new bride of the accused unfortunately was more beautiful and since the sexual advances of the contractor were repulsed by her, the husband of the newly wed was implicated by planting the piece of information recovered from his person while he was tilling his land. The case was ultimately closed and the accused allowed to go home honourably.

These are unusual situations and therefore unusual remedy too had to be sought. But the fact remains that but for the unethical methodology, we would have never succeeded in ascertaining the true facts of the case and the accused and his family would have suffered immensely.

Much can be said about for and against the employment of technological and chemical aids in the interrogation techniques but one of the most vital fact which emerges from the experience is that if we do so with fair and impartial mind, and truth is never sacrificed, it may beneficial for all, the suspect included.

6

Interrogation and Intelligence Gathering

There is a considerable amount of misconception that interrogation techniques are useful or should be employed only for a confessional statement with a view to secure a conviction against a criminal. In fact, the intelligence craft is an integrated medium and each of its components either compliments the other or it can be skilfully used to supplement the other component. In fact, unless until holistic approach is applied, the outcome may be fractured and distorted and at times irrelevant to the other components. We have been talking of the study of background material of a particular subject before the serious interrogation is undertaken. After all what is a background material and from where it is retrieved? Background material is valuable information decimated after days, months and years of painstaking efforts to prepare the database or an individual on a group of individuals or an organisation. Such intelligence can be gathered by launching of discreet surveillance operations, analysis of modes of financial transactions, sources of finance and interrogation of individuals who may not have any direct or positive role in the commitment of an offence. In fact, there is a saying in the Army that the best source of information about possibility of an imminent war is the Langar Commander, the equivalent of a chef of star hotel if we are fond of using the media phraseology. Infantry walks on its belly and first signs of war will start becoming visible when the rationing of the provisions starts at a considerable scale. On the same analogy, intelligence gathering has undisputable influence in the quality of interrogation and so is the case when the quality of interrogation will have very positive bearing on the intelligence gathering or in the ultimate aim of the interrogation. Thus, it is abundantly clear that each segment of the intelligence craft is like a step in the ladder, each being relevant and mutually complimenting the other. More often than not we loose sight of this vital phenomenon and futility of the efforts become not only visible but at times embarrassing too. Lapses continue to occur owing to faulty briefing, lack of co-ordination before an interrogation is resumed and to a larger extent our myopic approach to the issues at stakes. Debriefing or brain-storming sessions are seldom held and we continue to function in splendid isolation and poor results are there for all of us to see. It is a fact that the major aim of any interrogation is to establish the culpability of an accused very essential ingredient to ensure conviction of an accused in a court of law but at the same time, interrogation is very vital tool in developing very reliable intelligence database. We tend to ignore the potentiality of the interrogation techniques in intelligence gathering, may be because of the fact that it may not be of immediate concern. Knowledge is power and secret knowledge is a secret power and intelligence is nothing but this secret knowledge. We must remember that knowledge is not acquired in a span of short period but calls for painstaking, diligent work over a period of time. Huge wealth of information can be built up during the course of interrogation which can have far reaching influence in the crime detection or in averting a serious crime which may be likely to be committed.

I have never been a policeman, but in a wider context, every official connected with the enforcement action is naturally policing certain spheres of the criminal activity. Any individual who has been part of any investigative effort of the crime world would be inclined to think and retrospect two dismal failures of our policing efforts of virtually two decades. We have definitely gone wrong somewhere resulting into Veerappan and Dadua phenomenon as if these are mysterious characters from the other planet. There will be numerous others equally notorious who have escaped attention. Let us take the Veerappan first. (Since eliminated by the special task force of Tamil Nadu and Karnataka, nevertheless there shall be far too many Veerappan and the likes in future and thus remains relevant to over subject.

Veerappan is a living ghost made of flesh and blood, who like all of us breaths air, drinks water, eats food may be of good quality in terms of caloric value to keep himself and his gang operational and agile in inhospitable mountainous terrains and jungles. In contemporary criminal history no criminal drama has been staged with such brutality and that too so successfully for over fifteen years. It has left fifty plus persons dead including few valiant police officers, hundreds of elephants poached and thousands of sandalwood trees felled. The wounds of kidnapping of film icon Rajkumar were still in the process of healing, when Nagappa a former MLA was kidnapped. To add insult to the injury it had been reported by the media that a Doctor too had been kidnapped to take care of the ailing detenu which ultimately resulted into his tragic death after his body was recovered from Handigodusone forests 50 kms from Kamagere. Satyamanglam forests, the abode of Veerappan and neighbouring regions of Tamil Nadu bordering regions of Karnataka and Wyanad in Kerala have virtually become his exclusive territory where he roams freely, kills with impunity and mocks at the all powerful mighty Police forces of the two state governments by sending emissaries with recorded tapes outlining his strategy for his future well being. He is not satisfied with that much alone but also specifically names as to who should be the government emissary to secure the release of a particular detenu; one being a Tamil activist Kolathisr Mani lodged in Bellary jail in Karnataka and a local leader Mohadev Swamy. A time frame of eight days was also stipulated failing which threatening to harm Nagappa. The whole scenario brings out very salient features of his modus operandi :

(i) He is not living off the land and in fact nobody can survive for that length of time howsoever highly trained, motivated or hardened criminal one may be. The very fact that he could provide meals of choice to Nagappa, clearly indicates that he is not totally cut off from the world and made purchases from the local traders.

(ii) He is not only dependent on somebody for his daily needs of provisions but also has access to modern chemist and druggist stores to keep his hostage including himself in good shape for months together. After all he has to carry his hostages along with him to his constantly shifting hideouts.

(iii) He has vast and highly reliable intelligence network to communicate with the powers that be to convey his demands.

(iv) Demography of the region a mixed population of tribals and nomads speaking different dialects derived from Kannada, Tamil and Malayalam is also helpful to him. They all appear to be in awe against the terror of the bandit and their loyalty is easily purchased by him.

(v) Uninterrupted supply of recorded cassettes to the authorities cleverly indicates that there are many in the knowledge of his whereabouts.

(vi) The detenu in Bellary Jail appears to be much more knowledgeable about his whereabouts and there is likelyhood that he may be in communication with the bandit or is likely to get in communication whenever if and when the demand of Veerappan is conceded by the Authorities.

It is now very clear Veerappan is not living in isolation to carry out his criminal activities. He has a well defined geographical territory to roam freely and to carry out his nefarious activities without any fear. He has a dedicated band of operatives who cater for his logistics and well oiled network providing early warning of any likely police action.

The failure of the authorities to nab him dead or alive clearly indicates strategic intelligence failure and besides overt action which is resorted to whenever a kidnapping takes place, a silent, discreet and offensive strategy should have been devised long ago "to pierce his network by developing reliable intelligence on him. If an editor of a non-descript paper could time and again reach him in jungles why not the intelligence authorities and therefore interrogation of certain categories of individuals could provide us vital clues exposing his entire modus-operandi and thereby making him highly vulnerable to any swift lightening police action. The individuals who can be short listed for interrogation could be as under :

(i) Owners of provision and grocery stores in his areas of operation.

(ii) Owners of chemist shops of the area.

(iii) Dealers in arms and ammunition, as he has to replenish his stocks from time to time. This should include not only authorised dealers but also those engaged clandestinely in arms trafficking.

(iv) Persons engaged in money transaction business. In every village we do not find more than one or two of this category of persons. After all his illicit earning have to be siphoned off before the money bags become too heavy for him to carry on his back.

(v) Dealers in illegal trading of ivory and sandalwood and their conduits.

We are aware of the fact that at one time the strength of the Veerappan gang was reduced to three persons from a strong force of 150. Whenever overt police action was launched even if Veerappan gave a slip, effort should have been made to catch few members of the gang by capturing them alive. Unfortunately there is a tendency to shoot down the criminal forgetting that they are also treasure house of valuable intelligence. Emphasis should have been on physically incapacitating ensuring smooth retrieval of the wounded gang members for purposes of interrogation. After such preliminary pre-requisites, the sustained interrogation should have undertaken to ascertain maximum details about the man eluding the police and also the modus operandi which may cover the following broad parameters :-

(i) Life style of Veerappan.

(ii) General state of health specially those parameters which are likely to effect his mobility.

(iii) Food habits including likings for drinks or drugs.

(iv) Modes of communication with outside world. Even recently kidnapped Nagappa, a known MLA from Hanur are strangers to him. He is supposedly having links even with those serving jail terms and he must be using certain safe channels of communications to reach them to convey his ransom demands or for other favours.

(v) Tracking down flow of money earned by him illegally. After all he must not be shifting his conduits very often and must be banking with a trusted few.

(vi) Every criminal has a deity to worship. It is irony that prayers are directed to achieve the criminal goals but it is a fact and there is nothing unusual about it. In certain video clippings he has been offering prayers. It is likely that he may not personally visit his deity but surely some emissary must be going there to appease the deity. All devil forces are highly religious. They all derive strength from Ravana an ardent devotee of Shiva who did not hesitate to behead himself to acquire the destructive powers.

(vii) Last but not least the information on his sexual preferences, sexual escapades, concubines, temporary as well as permanent. It is most fragile and obsessive aspect of human traits and vital clues on his personal life if any, would have been of immense value to outwit him.

We have witnessed in Afghanistan that a mighty nation using most brutal force did succeed in ousting Taliban regime but could not lay hand on Osama-bin-Laden or his topmost aides neither dead nor alive., in spite of tall claims of smoking them out. It was primarily because the failure of human network of intelligence gathering. The Al Qaeda members taken during the operation are of no consequence since even to them Bin-Laden was a myth. The need of the hour was to get into the inner circle of Veerappan. The inner circle can be pierced by carefully planting the operatives in cover jobs by providing inducements to his trusted aides and by capturing his accomplices for sustained interrogation. This in no way can jeopardise an ongoing overt operations to get him and can be undertaken simultaneously. It is a fact that recently inducted National Security Guard in the Special Task Force had to be withdrawn since two state Governments had no intelligence on the whereabouts of Veerappan. It needs no emphasis that successful interrogation of one trusted lieutenant of Veerappan would have definitely puncture he myth of Veerappan.

Now let us shift to Sheo Kumar alias 'Dadua'. Yes the real name of 'Dadua' is Sheo Kumar. Unfortunately his village is very close to my native place in Banda District of Uttar Pradesh. I will not be surprised if he were a junior student in the college in some lower class where I studied. Dadua word is derived from word 'Dadu' a local dialect of Bundel Khandi and usually a growing boy is affectionately addressed as 'Dadu' by elders of the village. In fact, it is a common mode of addressing a younger person whose name you do not know as it immediately establishes a rapport. 'Dadua' is derivative of 'Dadu' and linguistically connotes the same except that in 'Dadua' genuine element of fear creeps in. Dadua specialised in kidnapping and extortion. The peculiar terrain of Banda district adjoining Chitrakut, Manikpur Blocks with forests of Madhya Pradesh have really proved to be a very fertile ground for his nefarious activities. During the last two decades special task force of Uttar Pradesh and Madhya Pradesh had been running after him without any success. He was very ruthless in killing and is very quick in physical elimination of persons who dare to give any information to the police about him. Though he patronised a particular caste to keep his criminal graph flourishing, yet he had no mercy for those who betray him, irrespective of the caste. For this very reason, in spite of the fact that the police of Uttar Pradesh and Madhya Pradesh had not been able to lay hand on him although crores of money has been spent to nab him. He was very shrewd, agile and disappears into thin air at the faint smell of the tracking police force.

The most striking difference between the two bandits is that unlike Veerappan, Dadua harbour a very strong ambition for himself to play a political role as well in future. With that end in view he intimidates the electorate in support of his proxies and surprisingly his front men win the election. It is not only the common voter to whom he intimidates but also those who are responsible for nominating the prospective candidates for any election for the state legislature or even Parliament. I know for definite, a class fellow of mine was nominated as a candidate for Lok Sabha election few years back on a ticket of a national political party and he spent fortunes to ensure his victory. Alas at the last minute his candidature was cancelled owing to threats of Dadua and a nominee of his choice was given a ticket who of course was elected. It would not have been surprising when he too like Phoolan Devi enter Parliament when he would be given a ticket as a reward for his relentless fight for the cause of downtrodden. Unlike, Veerappan he is visible but is adept in vanishing tricks leaving no trace of himself. There was no dearth of intelligence on him as it was is an open secret with vast network of sympathisers where he took shelter while on the run.

In view of the peculiar modus operandi of Dadua, probably a different strategy should have been worked out. In his case, the chase has to follow as a lightening action after the interrogation of his trusted accomplices in his crimes of kidnapping, extortion and murder. On the face of it, it looks simple but is difficult because time gap of interception of an accomplice, his interrogation and impending follow-up action of nabbing him, have to go in a swift chronological order with utmost secrecy. Although eliminated in police encounter yet shall ever remain relevant for are study.

It is imperative that we employ interrogation techniques as a major tool in developing intelligence on such bandits to ensure blockade of their escape routes and successfully smoke them out from the viceden where they have been hiding to ensure relief to the suffering humanity from their cruel hands. It may be pertinent to mention that Veerappan and Dadua have been singled out for special mention purely with a view to highlight the indifference of the society towards such criminals and the system-failure of the law enforcing agencies. There are numerous in the making that like cancerous cells are invisible and will explode some day. We have to have constant vigil, a long-term strategic vision for strengthening the intelligence network to eliminate incarnation of such dreaded criminals.

7

Interrogation and Vulnerability of a Criminal

In our great epic Ramayana there is a very important episode during the final stages of the battle between Lord Rama and demon king Ravana. Many fierce encounters in the battle field remained inconclusive and in spite of mighty strength of Lord Rama, the Ravana continued to remain invincible and it was a matter of great concern for the divine forces. The friendly interrogation of Vibhishan, the younger brother of Ravana who had crossed over to Lord Rama led to revelation of nectar in his biblic cord and then it transpired that the nectar reservoir had to be dried up first then only Ravana could be killed. It was a very vital piece of intelligence arising out of the interrogation of Vibhishan which lead to the knowledge that after all even Ravana was vulnerable in spite of his mighty strength which he had acquired. This fact is virtually eternal and every individual howsoever strong, motivated, indoctrinated and gritty one may be, there are bound to be certain and definite vulnerable traits in the total personality of a suspect which if ascertained in time can be of immense value for smooth and successful operation. The vulnerability of a suspect has to be identified by sustained interrogation and no piece of information should be discarded howsoever trivial it may appear prima-facie. With statutory requirement of producing a suspect within 24 hours of arrest the task of identifying vulnerable traits becomes rather difficult. We have a false notion of accounting the twenty four hours from the point of arrest. The Indian Penal Code does not make a distinction between a formal and informal arrest. If an individual's freedom is curbed, it tantamount to arrest although there may not be a formal document to corroborate it. Legally an illegal custody can be rightly construed to be an arrest. With such constraints we can draw curtain hypothetical parameters which can be of help to identify the vulnerability of a suspect. We should therefore seek answers in-depth in relation to the following questions :-

(i) Sensitivity of the suspect.

(ii) Emotional level of the suspect.

(iii) Religious background, training and level of indoctrination.

(iv) Personality traits revealing ego of the subject.

(v) Financial status and commitment of the subject.

(vi) Vulnerability to veiled threat of reprisals.

To identify the vulnerability of an individual one has to be a psychologist and sociologist - rolled into one, because these traits will manifest themselves automatically during the course of interrogation. It is a known fact that not getting the breakthrough in an interrogation is indeed a very frustrating experience, as it not only hampers the investigation but also gives an opportunity to the accused to overcome the stunning effect of having fallen into the dragnet. It is not unusual especially in respect of those suspects who usually frequent the jail very often, but also in respect of those with a very high degree of motivation. Any 'jail bird' is conscious of the limitations of the interrogator and is conscious of the fact that he has to be produced in the court within a mandatory time limit of twenty four hours and therefore skilfully dodges the thrust of investigation even veiled threats of physical reprisal does not produce the desired results for the simple reason of limitations of translating such threats in to some visible action.

It is also a known fact that we cannot expect an interrogation to be an amalgamation of all worldly wisdom to produce quick results. Experience has shown us that notwithstanding such limitation, we can draw certain lessons from our own or other's experience and can really achieve quick breakthrough. To bring home the methodology, few practical illustrations would be quite useful.

As referred to earlier, a highly qualified individual with a postgraduate degree who had a very decent family background was caught red handed in Delhi border when he escorted a truck load of smuggled synthetic fabric from Gujarat coast. As no breakthrough was forth coming with regard to syndicate leaders, financers and their modus operandi, he was strapped semi-naked, made to sit on the floor and directed to write his voluntary statement the way he liked. It deeply hurt his sensitivity because he could not reconcile to the humiliation. With tears in his eyes he requested for a chair and table which was promptly provided. To our surprise he gave out even the micro details about the whole chain of smuggling activities of his syndicate. Needless to say the swift-follow-up resulted into demolition of the entire syndicate.

It may be recalled that in the beginning itself there is a reference to one Pala Singh. Unfortunately for him he once sent his only son to collect the packet of smuggled gold being smuggled in by a British Airways flight in early hours. The boy did not know the seriousness of the situation as he was told that one uncle was bringing a parcel from London which will be delivered to the driver and he had simply to accompany the driver. A bright student of prestigious public school of Delhi, totally unaware of the consequences of his mission, he was loitering around in the outside area of the Airport casually. We were also unaware of his presence since no one had ever seen him in the past. No sooner the contraband gold weighing 34 kgs. was loaded in the car, it was intercepted and brought to Pala Singh's residence for follow-up action leaving the boy stranded at the airport. While the search was in progress the boy also walked in and informed his father that the car was taken away by certain unknown miscreants along with the driver.

Now this son was very dear to Pala Singh because all his hopes and aspirations were centred on him. He harboured a dream that he will give his child the best of education, which he himself never got and will make him a very respectable citizen of the society. His emotional attachment to his son came very handy to us to get a very early breakthrough as his attachment to his son was skilfully utilised to achieve a very faithful account of the entire network of his clandestine activities by air route. In any case the boy could not have been booked for the smuggling offence for lack of mens area, besides he was of tender age. Fortunately this boy later studied in London and currently Managing Director of his own multinational firm.

The case of Tanveer Hassan Awan, a young engineer, resident of Karachi in Pakistan is rather more amusing. He was suspected to have smuggled in approximately Rs.1.4 crores of contraband gold while he was employed in Mechanised Vessel BARZAN and was picked up from the ship for interrogation on 14th May, 1999 by the rummaging and intelligence division of the Mumbai Customs Preventive Commssionerate. It is difficult to get a confessional statement from a ship's crew of international shipping lines because they enjoy certain privileges which are not extended to local smugglers. During the course of interrogation it transpired that his mother hailed from a village of Banda District in Uttar Pradesh. Luck was also in our favour, since to his bad luck, I happened to be from that very district and his relations were immediately identified. This was identified as the most vulnerable aspect of his social kin-ship and made use of to the hilt. Fearing adverse social ramifications of non co-operation, he made very startling disclosures on assurance that his relatives in India should not be informed about his commission of crime and consequential preventive detention. The presence of his relatives in India may appear co-incidental but such situations surface before us far too many and must be exploited ruthlessly. It is human nature that they brag about their financial achievements to impress friends and relatives and become very vulnerable when caught on the wrong foot.

It is noticed that neo-rich who acquire higher financial status by dubious methods have feet of clay and carry the burden of very fat ego on their head and cannot reconcile to the misery where they have landed by their illicit activities. They therefore from the very beginning flaunt their financial status, political clout and bureaucratic links to overawe the interrogator. An interrogator should not get intimidated with such naked display of their connections and should go about in a professional manner. In fact, every opportunity should be availed to puncture their ego to convey the message that to us they are just another criminal. A so called very prominent citizen with a view to become billionaire resorted to false exports in connivance with his Dubai associates and succeeded in laundering Rs. 110 crores of black money besides defrauding exchequer to the tune of Rs. 15 crores by way of export incentives, within a span of five months before his rags consignments declared to certain fancy ladies dress material were seized by Mumbai Customs Preventive Commssionerate. During the entire course of interrogation, he threatened the interrogators that nothing would happen to him and on the contrary we would pay for our misdemeanours. Ultimately when he was arrested and directed to sign the arrest memo he refused unless until he was allowed to speak to a top bureaucrat in Delhi. He was crest fallen when informed that the person whom he wanted to speak had neither powers to arrest him or enlarge him on bail since such authority was invested in the Inspector who had arrested him and signed the arrest memo. The big balloon of inflated ego vanished in thin air and he immediately volunteered to proceed to Jail. Persons with such fat ego should however be allowed to have their say and should not be interfered till they have exhausted and should be struck at the right moment.

Invariably in all offences henchmen are recruited who do the job for their masters. They also belong to the lower economic strata and with unending financial liabilities. Since they are in total financial mess, they can easily be won over with inducements, false or real. After sustained interrogation, we converted a hard core accomplice of an Indian exporter at Dubai as our own informer because he was in doldrums financially and was getting roughly Rs. 4 lakhs against each consignment simply for dumping the consignments in the sea to destroy the evidence. He realised hefty amount of reward money more lucrative than what he was getting from his masters for illicit activities.

Religious sentiments play an important role in the development of an individual's personality. No religion preaches hatred or promotes crimes. A very interesting incident came to light when an American citizen was captured by US forces during the operations in Afghanistan who had joined the Taliban forces as a Jehadi (Crusader). Originally he was a Christian but had later converted to Islam. During the course of interrogation, he admitted his folly and futility of his self-assigned role and was sentenced to twenty years of imprisonment by a US court very recently. Though we are not in possessions of his disclosures but ostensibly his religious background prior to his conversion to Islam may have been instrumental in making the confessional statement. Back home persons caught in espionage activities do remain very vulnerable on religious count and this vulnerability should be exploited to the fullest degree. The voluntary confessions of Hansi Cronje, the erstwhile South African Cricket Captain also points out the same facts which ultimately resulted in unearthing of Cricket match fixing.

Every criminal, economic offender or falling in other categories of crime, embrace crime with definite aim of providing financial security to his dependants and also a social status which is now an easily purchasable commodity. During the interrogation proceeding such relations can be easily identified. During the course of interrogation if a subject proves to be a hard nut to crack veiled threats should be given to the accused creating an impression that the consequences of non-cooperation would be very disastrous for his near and dear ones. A very interesting case of solving hundreds of burglaries by Delhi Police appeared in national print media. The victims of this Bunty were from very affluent society residing in posh colonies of Delhi. The total burglaries aggregating in the range of one hundred crores. It must have been a cake walk for Delhi Police since the disclosure were made against a veiled threat that his girl friend with whom he was emotionally involved too shall be roped in. The veiled threat paid the rich dividends, totally unexpected and confessional disclosure started coming out like a printed sheet of paper from computer.

There may be a situation where a criminal may be totally immune to such probable vulnerability. There is no need to get frustrated since there is no person who is not vulnerable on some count or the other. The quest to identity the 'Achilles Heel' should continue with more vigil and zeal and at some point of time one is definitely going to identify the reservoir of nectar which can be evaporated by intelligent and sustained interrogation.

8

Joint Interrogation

Modern day crime has assumed a very complex scenario. It is no more an act attributable to a single individual or a local syndicate but has really gone global. Take for example the illicit trade in the narcotics and psychotropic substances, hawala operations, contractual killings by mafia gangs or extortions racket, the networks of all these clandestine operations are spread over many countries across the world and are efficiently administered by best of the infrastructure and logistic back up. Mafia leaders engaged in contractual killing have a well established rank hierarchy, well defined pay structure based on the merit and utility of the gang member. Many will be surprised to know that during the last clemency of voluntary disclosure of income under the Income Tax, one Mafia leader of Mumbai specialising in extortion popularly called 'hafta' made a disclosure of Rs. 4 crores under the Scheme, although he was never engaged in any legitimate economic activity and most of the times was lodged in jail. In the case of Dawood syndicate known as D-company, the annual turn over in trading runs over many thousand crores, of course the initial investment going into such trade was earned by all illicit activities of murders, extortions and Hawala operations. Hawala operators no more function for the lure of the money but they are very vital components of terrorist gangs because they want to have the utmost confidentiality in their money transactions. These are not mere simple transactions but lot of effort is put together to achieve a well defined short term as well as long term strategy. Money laundering is no more a tool of converting black money into white money but is aimed at achieving very sinister goals. Even licit trading channels are extensively used for money laundering.

With such dangerous scenario, the plethora of intelligence agencies who are used to act independently of each other rather than in tandem, fail to get into the root cause and therefore demolishing of a syndicate has only a superficial impact in the context of the existing network of the operators of the crime. We pathetically lack a holistic vision to contain the menace, which continues to grow as the crime graphs amply suggest. Unfortunately there is no concept of joint interrogation except in theory and every agency is working in splendid isolation and patting it's own back for whatever little success they achieve.

What do we understand by the Joint Interrogation? Does it mean sending an unwilling individual to some other department as a ritual with no responsibility or accountability? Does it mean simply completing a formality? The answers is a No. It is high time we come out with institutional arrangements, more so at grass-root level because it is the field officer who holds the key to achieve desired results and analyst can do the job efficiently only when the fidelity of the inputs of the interrogation are unquestionable.

The pertinent question is what are the reasons of falling to evolve a cohesive approach and whether institutional arrangements have to be given a mandatory requirement to go about the job. The full import of the consequences of lack of institutional arrangements for carrying out joint interrogation cannot really be imagined if we speak only theoretically. The gravity of lack of such formal arrangements unfortunately is never comprehended fully by who run the show. It can best be conveyed by narrating few live situations encountered in the past during the interrogation. Let us take only two or three examples.

There was the case of one Fida Hussain (assumed name) a Saudi Arabian national operating from Gulf Emirates. He goes to London, withdraws from his bank account sterling pounds equivalent to Rs. One crore, comes to India stays few days in Delhi, goes to Dehradun and then to Bangalore. After a week flies back to London, stays there for one week and then again comes back to Mumbai in December, 1997 and stays in a non-descript hotel in a busy locality of Mumbai near Victoria Terminus railway station. To his bad luck this time he is intercepted in the Hotel by Mumbai Customs Preventive Commssionerate. Brand new sterling pounds with London bank seal equivalent to Rs. 36 lakhs smuggled clandestinely are recovered and seized. Nothing very startling, since it was a modest recovery and routine affair as we witness such seizures far too often in Mumbai and Delhi. Let us see the inventory of other items recovered:

(i) Passport issued by the Saudi Arabian authorities.

(ii) Passport issued by the Indian Passport authorities which he obtained under an assumed Hindu name.

(iii) Driving licence issued by Saudi Arabian authorities.

(iv) International driving licence.

(v) Driving licence issued by the Indian authorities against the assumed Hindu name as shown in the Indian passport.

(vi) One photo album containing photographs with a girl purported to be his girl friend from Dehradun.

(vii) Pocket size stainless steel handcuff. These hand cuffs are neither manufactured nor available in India. Even abroad these are sold only to police officers and defence personnel.

I had managed to purchase one in Singapore in 1991 for my office with the co-operation of the Military Attache in the High Commission who incidentally was known to me, otherwise he too would have never obliged. Foreigners buying such handcuff have to give an undertaking that it shall not be used in the host country where the purchase was being made.

He had explanations for every thing, although totally false and unconvincing and unfortunately we could probe only to a limited extent, since the questions had to be carried out under various different statutes necessitating handling of the subject by other agencies and even Interpol. Unfortunately no agency responded to us and we had to contend only with his preventive detention for a period of one year. No one knows what we have lost for lack of joint interrogation.

There was another syndicate specialising in false exports of chemicals and garments. They were very conversant of the system and procedural flow of export documentation and thus successfully forged the documents which showed the export value in the range of 110 crores although the intrinsic value of the exports may not have been more than five to ten crores. It is inconceivable that any prudent businessman abroad will remit the money through banking channels for the cargo not received. Even before such forged documents were created seventy percent of the inward remittances were made by one Abdul Razak, a notorious smugglers and Mafia leader from Pakistan operating from Dubai. The question arises as to why he was doing so. How such huge finances were being diverted by him without being beneficiary of any export goods from India. He could have been a ISI operative or an agent of some fundamentalist outfit engaged in surveillance activities and may have build up huge fortunes by such clean operations for terrorist funding in India. A joint interrogation was the need of the hour but that was not to be.

Let us look into the third scenario. A garment exporter exported over 100 consignments of Rags by declaring these to be ladies garments between January, 2000 and May, 2000 and received the inward remittance of over Rupees one hundred crores although the value of the shipments may not have been more than a crore or two. The consignee in this case at Dubai was one Muslim gentleman of dubious antecedents. The most amusing part was his firm at Dubai.

Functioned under the name and style of "Nirvana Trading Co." deriving inspiration from Vedantic philosophy.

Now these are the typical cases which were detected by Mumbai Customs Preventive Commissionerate in a very short period of two to three years and at all India level the figures may be alarming. The damage such illegitimate transactions using legitimate channels cause cannot be really quantified.

It appears to be inborn trait of our psyche that we prefer to work in isolation. Hijackers of Indian Airlines plane from Kathmandu only a few years back could therefore get Passports and Driving Licences from Indian authorities whereas a bonafide Indian citizen may run from pillar to post for the same. Fully knowing that there is huge potential in joint interrogations, such opportunities are either lost or ignored, sometimes wilfully and most of the time by our own sheer indifference why bother, it is somebody else's baby - that is our attitude. There is a very appropriate proverb in Hindi language which defines our mindset very fittingly, i.e., 'Aath Kanaujia Nau Chulhe' which if translated loosely in English would mean and connotes 'eight persons from Kanauj - a district of western Uttar Pradesh will always have nine kitchens'. We refuse to work in co-ordination with others, because we always fear our performance will get diluted. I know of a case where one intelligence outfit wanted to know the deployment of customs personnel engaged in anti-smuggling operations. The information was not made available on the grounds that it will seriously jeopardise the operational achievements of the customs outposts. After their vain efforts for some time they gave up the idea for information which I am sure they must have got from their own sources along with the bio-data and authentic write up on propensities of the officers manning the outpost.

It is not the point that every case should undergo the regime of the joint interrogation because it will drain the resources and would become counter productive. Certain guidelines can be formulated taking into consideration of the ramifications of the case and some agency can be designated as nodal agency to co-ordinate and oversee the progress. Officers from different agencies having working knowledge of various disciplines can be nominated sufficiently in advance for a stipulated period to constitute the joint Interrogation team. It is unavoidable necessity and we can remain aloof only at our own peril.

9

Faulty Interrogation and Comedy of Errors

Strictly speaking intelligence craft cannot be compartmentalised. It is a composite whole and each component in one way or the other supplements to its totality which in turn emerges as a total intelligence scenario. In our usual understanding it is our perception that interrogation is primarily carried out to pin down an accused so that the prosecution could be launched against him. In a limited sense it is true but interrogation can also be an important tool in intelligence gathering to enable us to understand the complexity of a crime. Interrogation thus assumes more importance in the entire game plan of intelligence craft. In this context an interesting episode needs narration. Sometimes in way back July, 1988 two highly educated but unemployed youth hailing from Varanasi landed in the office of a prominent Cabinet Minister in Delhi. They had a very interesting intelligence up their sleeves which was conveyed by them as under :

The Mughal Emperor Aurangzeb while returning from Deccan campaign in South India when he was passing through Gazipur district of eastern Uttar Pradesh en route to Delhi buried in deep earth two brass Handas (large receptacle used in olden days to conceal treasures under the earth) filled with roughly 100 Sers (now roughly corresponding to 100 kilograms) gold Asharfis, where now exist a small village called Bhitri Bazar, approximately three to four kilometres off Varanasi-Gazipur Highway. He chose this place since there was a pillar with edicts of emperor Ashok of great Mauryan Empire and was easily identifiable. Such practice may have existed since such concealed treasure was always handy as a back-up wealth for future campaigns in distant lands and also relatively secured against possible loot of the Mughal treasure by Maratha invaders. Bhitri Bazaar a small township of about 5000 inhabitants existed in the site and a house was supposedly constructed by a shopkeeper over the buried treasure and it was a shop-cum-residence of the businessman, who did not know that he was sleeping on treasures. Hand made sketch of the house drawn by these informers was also furnished giving the exact location of the priceless treasures. Since the subject matter was beyond the purview of the Minister they were guided to the then Finance Minister with a request for immediate follow-up action. The crack sleuths of the Central Economic Intelligence Bureau were entrusted with the task and I was designated as the ground level leader of the mission. I was selected not because there were no better officers but die was cast in my favour, as I was familiar with regional dialect, an asset to launch an operation in the interior countryside. I was excited as I was going to get an opportunity to visit Udai Pratap College, Varanasi - an alma meter of my late father. He had an intense desire that I should do my graduation from that college as he always used to narrate stories of his days in school with glee in his eyes specially how he had donated fifty-one rupees to his school from his savings from the money of monthly money order of seven rupees way back in 1920 and his names was inscribed in the stone pillars of the donors. His dream was never fulfilled as he could not afford the expenses of my graduation level studies in Udai Pratap College.

Planning an operation in countryside requires special care unlike in cities where each individual is anonymous to the other. Any inkling of an intended operation would have blown the lid rendering the whole effort futile. Cover of students of Ancient History of Delhi University was assumed. To merge with the crowd ready made Paijama Kurta etc. were purchased from the Khadi Emporium and armed with cameras, recording devices we landed at Bhitri Bazar. Every one jettisoned snobbishness and casual clumsy and careless front was created to gain credibility. Reconnaissance was carried out in a most convincing manner and we also managed to have a cup of tea from the owner of the house intended to be searched.

On return to Delhi, after debriefing it was decided that we should also have a metal detector capable of locating the precious metal below earth since gold has a tendency not only to sink but also shift its position. An officer was flown to Ahmedabad and a huge metal detector was taken on loan from the Geological Survey of India. To us it looked more like a guitar or musical instrument than a metal detector.

Just before the launch of the operation one of our superior officer from Indian Police Service of UP Cadre, suggested that in case a recovery was made, the value of the centuries old coins owing to its historical significance and numismatic value would be in the range of rupees two hundred crores and therefore it was imperative that the entire operation be launched in co-ordination with the local police as there was every possibility that thousands of the spectators from the neighbouring villages will converge at the site and the recovery could be looted by the unmanageable crowd. It was really a brilliant idea and possibility of such incident taking place could not be ruled out altogether. As a logical corollary, the Dy. Inspector General of Varanasi range was also roped in who readily agreed to divert a battalion of Provincial Armed Constabulary and volunteered to oversee the operation on the ground on D day. A huge shamiana was erected on the Varanasi-Gazipur State Highway and make-shift kitchen was made operational to cater for the food of the workforce, no sooner than the entire village was cordoned off by the armed police.

To the surprise of the entire village the sleuths of the Central Economic Intelligence Bureau entered the house in full strength in search of the treasure. The interior lay out of the residence was identical to what was conveyed to us in the intelligence report. This fact really raised high hopes of striking the gold and the entire team thus got highly charged. The digging of the room where the treasure was purported to be concealed commenced at 8 a.m. and continued till 2 p.m. There was no sign of brass handas and our metal detector also maintained stony silence. Fortunately, both the informers also had accompanied us to the site and they were also directed to go deep down and join the digging team. This precaution was taken to eliminate the possibility of the informers going to the Minister again with some fabricated story. When the informer realised that too deep digging has been carried out and there was a possibility of roof collapsing over them, instead of themselves becoming a buried treasure, they pleaded to call off the digging and the operation at 3 p.m. in the afternoon. Crest fallen we all returned to the base camp at Varanasi empty handed.

Consequent upon failure of the operation it was decided at the top level to interrogate the informers to find out the real facts. It was even more delicate job as we were fully conscious of the fact that both the informers enjoyed very close clout with the Minister they had approached initially. We also did not want to miss the treasure in case the intelligence was really true. Sympathising with them by highlighting with their loss of fortunes by way of reward money we got their full co-operation and on sustained interrogation very amusing facts came to surface.

Varanasi is not only famous for the abode of Lord Shiva but also Bhairav an incarnation of the Lord. Wherever there is a God, self styled Sadhus claiming to be in communication with the Lord also mushroom. They grab a piece of land in a prime location, install Bhairav and then there is no looking back in the business. In local lingua-franca such places are called 'Aughad Baba Ki Takiya' which is rather difficult to be translated in English language but may connote resting place of Lord Bhairav. The head of such Ashram is always held in reverence and awe owing to his knowledge of Tantra vidya, which they employ to redress the grievance of the hapless individuals by making false promises. Our informers had made the place their permanent residence and they made constant efforts to please the Aughad Baba to strike fortune somewhere. Ultimately head of the Ashram performed some rituals and the informers were narrated a story which they furnished in the form of intelligence report to the Government believing it to be true and as they had witnessed the rituals when the Aughad Baba was in communication with Lord Bhairav in a state of trance. To an impartial observer it may be an amusing incident and one may enjoy it as comedy of errors but to a professional outfit it was an acute embarrassment. It was a colossal waste of manpower besides money spent on executing the mission. In retrospect, we can only laugh at ourselves. Why not at the first instance, the informers were interrogated at length to ascertain the reliability of the information which in any case was undertaken ultimately.

The whole incident raises certain very fundamental questions which underlines the importance of the interrogation in the composite scheme of intelligence craft. First and foremost requirement is- that at no stage professionalism should be sacrificed notwithstanding that the directions were from the highest quarters. It is incumbent upon the field officers to go into finer details by undertaking a comprehensive interrogation to verify the credibility of any information. Had we done that and brought to the notice of the superiors, the operation may not have been launched at all. Interrogation is our indispensable tool in intelligence craft and we should employ it without any hesitation instead being swayed away by extraneous and irrelevant considerations.

Part–II

Indian law enforcement agencies do not have the luxury (pun intended) of the freedom of action as those enjoyed by the CIA or the FBI of the USA who dump their detainees in metal strapping in containers fortified by layer of concertina wires where an accused is kept standing or kneeling for hours or held in awkward, painful positions, without sleep for days together with bombardment of lights round the clock. Stress and duress are the hallmarks of their interrogation techniques. We appear to be more civilised and our watchdogs are more pro-active when it is the question of human rights violation. However, extraordinary situations call for extraordinary approaches and methodology. In reality a contingency may arise when our conventional thinking, knowledge and expertise may not match with the complexity of a criminal's mind set and thus the necessity of unconventional innovative approach becomes inevitable.

Prima-facie the idea may be repugnant to a copy book fashion interrogator but at the end of the day when the mystery is solved resulting in an innocent being given clean chit or a guilty person making a suo-motto confession, the whole exercise is more than rewarding. Here are only a few awkward encounters from the archives of my memory where numerous such unorthodox events are carefully stored - some embarrassing but fruitful nonetheless.

10

One Quintal of Gold in Dustbin

It was 16th August, 1997. Intelligence was developed to the effect that a merchant ship "Tanscord" will be arriving Mumbai on the following morning and it was likely to smuggle 100 kgs. of contraband gold. There were also indications that the gold may be handed over to fishing boats in mid-stream off 40 kms. from Mumbai harbour to evade interception by the Preventive Commissionerate of Mumbai Customs. The ship was slated to anchor at about 5 a.m. the morning before entering into the harbour.

The sleuths of Rummaging and Intelligence Wing of the Preventive Commissionerate popularly called 'Black Gang' therefore swung into action. It was therefore decided to mount surveillance at sea to eliminate possibility of gold being off loaded to any fishing boat. Two speed boats of the Commissionerate were therefore put into action. It was heavily raining, the sea was choppy and the visibility very poor. We had taken into consideration about deteriorating weather conditions and one helicopter of the Commissionerate was in position at Juhu Airport to take off. Unfortunately the pilot could not take off which made the job still difficult. But weather could not prove deterrent to highly motivated and well trained team of the black gang and they boarded the ship at 6 a.m. in the morning 40 kms. off Bombay Harbour. Even the Master of the ship a German national was highly surprised by our crazy action and in private advised politely not to venture similar boarding in future as it was very risky. The ship was brought ashore where a thorough rummaging could be undertaken to recover the gold.

It is not a child's play to locate 100 kgs. contraband gold in a ship weighing over 30,000 tonnes with equal tonnes of cargo. In a seven story ship the task is something like finding a needle in a stack of straw. Anyway systematic rummaging was undertaken after allocating various segments of the ship to respective teams. After days of hard work ultimately the gold was found in a dustbin covered with waste material and food left-outs of the dinning hall. Recovery of the contraband gold did boost the morale of the rummaging team but it cast greater responsibility and challenge to identify and connect the individual to the crime failing which the purpose of anti-smuggling operation is defeated since the syndicate and its associates go scot-free as the gold originating from Dubai for being smuggled into India is insured and there is hardly any financial loss to the smugglers.

A very difficult if not impossible task lay ahead. There is hardly any gain if the offender is not pinned down and the seizure irrespective of the quantum looses much of its importance and relevance. After going through the first phase of process of elimination, it transpired that the culprit was one of the seventeen members of the crew mostly in lower order of the hierarchy who are usually lured to act as a carrier.

Interrogation becomes easier if the recovery is made from a person or from the premises occupied or under control of an individual. In instant case the gold was dumped in the dustbin owing to certain background prior to this seizure. Firstly, the sleuths of the Mumbai Customs Preventive Commissionerate had made a seizure of Rupees Three Crores of gold from another merchant ship of the same shipping line on 14th August, only forty eight hours earlier. Since every ship is now fitted with satellite telephone facility, the message of earlier seizure may have been conveyed to them. Secondly, the carriers did not want to get identified to evade the consequences of the law and had dumped the gold in the dustbin. Thirdly, there was a chance that rummaging team would not suspect such huge quantity of gold in a dustbin and if undetected, it could easily have been delivered to the recipient later. First and foremost action was therefore to detain the ship and therefore the ship valued at Rs. 34 crores was seized for transporting the contraband gold. This gave ample time to the department to get the confessional statement from the real accused and for carrying out further follow-up action.

It was a Herculean task to interrogate seventeen crew members, because security of suspects was equally important, since there is known tendency on the part of the suspects to resort to inflict injuries on self to turn the tables. Records of custodial death and grievous injuries witnessed in the past bear enough testimony where the department ran for cover for none of their faults. Thus, the interrogation process was like a grand mela approximately forty officers converging in one place to do the job. To our good luck all the crew members were Philippine and understood English language. The other saving grace was that the department did not suffer from any legal infirmities since the ship was under seizure and under our constant surveillance and the crew could be summoned and sent back to the ship at the end of the day. But the department was handicapped owing to certain privileges enjoyed by the crew members under international statutory conventions. The entire interrogation had to be carried out in the presence of authorised Advocate of the shipping line. The presence of the Advocate although of symbolic significance nevertheless was advantageous to the alleged suspects. Days passed by but no breakthrough was forthcoming - a very frustrating experience for any interrogator. We were virtually at the dead end with no hope of even identifying the suspect, leave alone any confessional statement from the offender. As a logical corollary a brain storming session was held to chalk out a workable strategy and the scenario unfolded as narrated below.

A medium size hall was grilled with iron rods with locking facility, all electrical lights and fans were removed and thick coloured curtains put in the enclosure. Pictures of religious Gods of different faiths were hung and the enclosure was named as 'Meditation Centre'. It was a fragile alibi to ensure the enclosure could not be construed as a lock-up centre which revenue department is not authorised to have. In any case it could be used as a bonafide yoga centre when not put to more useful purpose of interrogation. One day all seventeen crew members were summoned, directed to remove their shoes, shirts and vests and ushered in the meditation centre and locked from outside. No one spoke a word to them. By evening they were taken out and allowed to report to their ship. On day two they were directed to remove their pants and left inside the meditation centre. It had visible psychological effect as they were bewildered by such unusual approach. On the third day the same exercise was carried out but this time each suspect was taken out one by one and was informed in very certain terms that enough was enough and they should now be prepared to face the most crucial phase as an AIDS infected patient's services from the red light areas were hired and each one will be exposed to AIDS menace. A volunteer lady official appeared in the scene for a while and also walked in with a video-graphy team with video camera and other equipments. A veiled threat was given that the proceedings of the final day activities will be filmed and video clipping sent to their homes as the department had all the passports and addresses. At the end of the day they were allowed to go home.

We were informed that a big fight took place on board ship during the night amongst the seventeen crew members and the two culprits were forced to own the offence to save the innocents the agony and fatal consequences of contracting AIDS for the offences which they had never committed.

On day four all appeared again. Most of them were cheerful and brimming with confidence except the two. Once again no word was spoken by the interrogators and the two who looked dejected and crest fallen gave a very detailed and credible voluntary statement good enough to justify their detention under the relevant statutory Act and also securing conviction as and when the prosecution was launched.

11

The Heroin Connection

It was some time in May, 1986 when Tony (assumed name) from Ludhiana was apprehended when he was intercepted by the officers of the Delhi Zonal Unit of the Directorate of Revenue Intelligence while coming out from the lobby of a five star hotel. Only a few hours earlier he had deposited one kg. of pure heroin for safe custody for a night in the residence of one of his contact man in Jangpura colony of New Delhi. The heroin was duly seized by the officers and it was during the spot interrogation that Tony figured as the main man resulting in his interception. It was very unusual of a syndicate leader to carry the substance himself since trusted members of the gang recruited for the job invariably carry out such assignments. It was, therefore, understandable that he delinked himself from the material for the night since he was expecting the foreign buyer to check-in to the same hotel on the following day. It was also likely that the foreign buyer was a high profile customer and in his first deal he may have disliked the idea of dealing with anybody else other than the leader of the cartel. Thus, Tony was taken into custody for detailed interrogation in the Headquarters.

In a pre-scheduled assignment, the services of the officers of the Revenue Intelligence were already diverted at the disposal of Central Economic Intelligence Bureau which had already planned a state wide Income Tax searches in the Kashmir Valley as well as Jammu region resulting in depleted strength of the Delhi Zonal Unit.

Notwithstanding manpower constraints the interrogation was entrusted to a very senior and competent officer as cases relating to narcotic drug offences are relatively difficult to crack owing to very harsh punishment in the event of clinching evidence. It was a challenging assignment since the suspect was highly sophisticated, well educated and very affluent financially. Under no circumstances it was going to be a cake walk as it was natural that the syndicate leader would not give up easily.

After a gap of four days the personnel diverted to J&K returned to office and to their surprise found Tony still in the office. The officer entrusted to head the interrogation team had taken his job too seriously which was quite visible from his grown beard, dirty clothes and sleepy eyes. Unfortunately for him no breakthrough had been achieved permanently because he had only skeleton staff at his disposal besides for obvious reasons he had no officers left to constitute the requisite interrogation teams. He was visibly relieved since he could go home, have much deserved bath and few hours of siesta. The interrogation team was therefore re-enforced and re-constituted to achieve the desired results. The detachments returning from the J&K were in high morale and feeling very important as for the first time they were part of an airborne operation undertaken by the Revenue Intelligence Department in its history.

The exercise was therefore undertaken afresh starting on a clean slate. During the in-depth interrogation very interesting layers of the personality of the subject were revealed. He appeared to be a man of highly refined tastes bordering aristocracy and loved his privacy immensely. He could not compromise on these counts. These traits may have been the reasons that no breakthrough was achieved. To take stock of the situation a brainstorming session was organised and it was decided to convert these strong traits of his personality into his weakest points to ensure that he gives up the resistance.

Well-conceived tactics were therefore worked out and a television set was installed in the hall of the main office along with VCR, ostensibly for the purpose of screening of a pornographic video film. The lady officers of the zonal unit were politely asked to go home and rest. Office premises were converted into makeshift mini-film theatre and for the staff it was very amusing experience to have a screening of the film that too in office hours. Of course very select few knew as to what was the film about.

A selected officer who had developed some rapport with the suspect was directed to convey to Tony about the contents of the film and further that he was going to be stripped naked and made to watch the film while standing in the centre of the hall amidst all the officers. The ploy had a devastating effect on his ego and he requested to be spared the humiliation in return for his confessional statement. Not a single frame of the film was ever played on the television screen since there was no pornographic film for the purpose, however a confessional statement giving graphic account, reconstructing the entire sequence was on our table. Only regret was that the foreigner supposed to collect the heroin could not be traced as he could not contact Tony who was cooling his heels elsewhere.

12

The Ladies Garments

Durjan Exports were supposedly leading exporters of garments of Mumbai going by infrastructure and by the strength of 200 Tailors purported to have been employed by the firm, one is tempted to believe the high profile business status of the firm engaged in earning valuable foreign exchange for the country. The firm was managed by the members of the family whose bio-data also appeared to be very impressive since most of them had management degrees from the United States and one of them even a Green Card holder. With such high credentials it was quite natural they had sufficient clout in political and also in bureaucratic hierarchy. Unfortunately these favourable circumstances were the very cause of their downfall since the clout they enjoyed made them arrogant and generated unchained greed for fast money. The false belief further resulted into false notion that they were above the law and no government machinery would ever be able to catch them.

As a logical follow-up action on receipt of very specific intelligence inputs to the effect that the firm was going to export eight consignments of rags declaring these to be ladies fancy skirts all the consignments were intercepted while these were being loaded for export by a chartered flight to Dubai. It was a risky decision since there was hardly any time to develop functional intelligence and instances of false intelligence inputs owing to professional rivalries are also very common in the trade. Infructuous results of examination of the cargo would have caused lot of embarrassment for the hasty action. Further, officers could also be hauled up for undue harassment to the so-called reputed exporters. We kept our fingers crossed. The exports documents categorically indicated that these were ladies fancy garments and the value of all eight consignments comprising over 1000 packages was declared to be over Rupees Eight Crores.

The Government of India has many lucrative export promotion incentives one of which is Duty Drawback Scheme, where an exporter gets cash incentives at prescribed rate linked to the FOB value of the export consignment. The intended purpose of Duty Drawback Scheme is to reimburse to the exporter the duty of inputs on the material which has gone into the manufacturing of the export product. Such incentive vary from item to item however it is quite high for the garment industry and in instant case if they had succeeded in effecting the export they would have straightway got a cheque of Rs.1.5 crores under the duty drawback scheme. The simultaneous search in the office premises resulted into export documents indicating export of 110 consignments between January - May, 2002, showing cumulative export value in the range of Rs.110 crores in which a duty back in the range of over Rs.12 crores had already been availed by the exporting firm. To aid to our anxiety the packing of the cargo was excellent and of international standards and no one could hazard even a guess of the contents thereof.

In view of the delicate scenario, the Mumbai Cusoms Preventive Commissionerate deployed a huge strength of over one hundred officers for speedy cent per cent thoough examination of the cargo. It was unprecedented action since the export consignments are treated like a holy cow and ramifications of false results too would have been unprecedented. For the exporter too it was an unprecedented situation as in their wildest dreams they had never bargained for such experience.

The entire cargo of over 1000 cartons was found to contain rags neatly packed in polythene coverings. Each skirt was made of cut-piece of an old and worn out sari averaging 10 to 15 inches in length and approximately 8 to 12 inches in width. These skirts could not be used even as a duster in an office owing to its size which was made of virtually rotten material. The export value of the total consignment was big zero because no expenses were incurred by the exporters except for the packing material of card board boxes, printed labels etc. and of course the labour. Had the chartered plane taken off the government could have been defrauded by Rs. 1.5 crores.

One would feel elated by having effected such a spectacular seizure and save the huge tax payer money which would have gone down the drain. But for us it was a situation like catching a snake's tale which is inside a hole. A very unpleasant experience even for those snake catchers who are engaged in this hereditary profession. Many vital questions were thrown on our face which needed answers :

(i) Why some one was paying such huge amounts by way of inward remittance against such false exports.

(ii) What the consignee was doing with such rags which had no value and zero utility.

(iii) The presumptions that past consignments too were rags would not hold water in any departmental adjudication proceedings or in any court of law for want of corroborative evidence thus making the recovery of fraudulently obtained drawback impossible for earlier false exports.

(iv) Are certain consignments still lying in Dubai uncleared, which could be recalled to ensure clinching evidence.

(v) Could any airline give us the credit facility if the consignments are lying uncleared at Dubai as sanction of money by the Department to recall these consignments is time consuming and any delay would have definitely resulted into destruction of evidence.

(vi) Was it feasible to interrogate the accomplice in Dubai to re-construct the sequence of events to quantify the consequential loss of revenue to the national exchequer owing to false exports and fraudulent claims of the drawback availed by the exporters from earlier consignments.

All the perpetrators of the offence were arrested and in due course the Government also passed the orders for their detention under Conservation of Foreign Exchange and Prevention of Smuggling Activities (COFEPOSA).

An uphill task began now onwards. To our surprise only Pakistan Airline and Ethiopian Airways agreed to airlift uncleared consignments from Dubai on credit basis out of all the flights operating in and out of Mumbai. Since the terms of Ethiopian Airlines were more economical their services were availed. They had however put a rider that subsequent consignments would be lifted only after the freight payment was received against each past bill. We could not keep the promise since the sanction for payment was taking time and situation in Dubai was getting too hot for us and thus only a few uncleared consignments could be recalled.

Information was received to the effect that a very influential emissary was sent from India by the firm to get the consignments cleared out of Dubai customs area. The emissary was duly empowered to use coercive methods and also inducement of money for such facilitation. In fact luck was favouring us as Dubai Customs were celebrating their Customs Centenary and the few consignments remained uncleared. To aid to the miseries of the exporter, the First Secretary (Economic) in our Consulate was known to me since we had a tenure together in an intelligence set up in the Revenue Department. He had very good working rapport with the Dubai Customs and he effectively got the further clearances blocked with the positive assistance of the Dubai Customs.

Luckily the few consignments of over 100 cartons recalled from Dubai by the Ethiopian Airlines contained nothing but the rags identical to those seized earlier in India. It strengthened our reasonable belief that the entire 110 shipment exported earlier too was also rags. There were still a number of consignments of 1000 cartons lying uncleared in Dubai Customs godowns. Even if examined this tally would still be short of entire shipments during the last five months. The stakes were too high. In fact the total drawback amount claimed from the Government fraudulently against exports of rags would have equalled to over Rs. 3.5 quintals smuggled contraband of gold. By any criteria, a scam of roughly Rs. 15 crores by a single exporter in a short span of five months is not a matter which could be taken lightly. It was therefore decided to send a team of officials to Dubai to examine the uncleared consignments and also interrogate the front man acting as bonafide consignee who was instrumental in destroying the evidence of bogus shipments. Interrogating a person abroad notwithstanding the fact that he was a Indian citizen was the biggest road block but a strategy had to be worked out to give it a different colour and interrogate him surreptitiously, inducing the suspect to believe that everything was being done to safeguard his interests. The ploy worked.

Over 1000 cartons lying uncleared were therefore examined jointly by the officers of Dubai Customs, Indian Customs officers of Mumbai Customs. Preventive Commissionerate in the presence of Indian Embassy officials at Dubai. Here again all uncleared consignments contained only rags of really no commercial value exactly identical to those seized in India.

It was therefore imperative to interrogate Fida Hussain (assumed name), the proprietor of the Durgati Trading Corporation, Dubai to unearth the entire modus operandi, since it was very essential to ensure such scams do not recur in future. Though Fida Hussain was cornered and the die was cast against him yet expecting a confessional statement from his was hoping far too much owing to heavy odds against the visiting Indian Customs team. But the officers deputed for the difficult task rose to the occasion and really did a commendable job.

Fida Hussain although a non-resident Indian besides business interest had other stakes as well in India and this fact was exploited to the hilt. Veiled threats and inducements were the only two weapons in our armoury to win him over and it really worked. He was made to believe that he was in a dark tunnel with no end in sight as he was told in uncertain terms that besides the proceedings under the Custom Act cases under the Indian Penal Code will also be slapped on him under the Prevention of Corruption Act for entering into criminal conspiracy with the Indian exporters to defraud the government. He was also made to believe that he will be black listed thereby completely sealing his business links with other Indian exporters which he could ill afford.

Even this was not sufficient in the event he admitted his role. What was relevant as material evidence was to bring on record as to what goods were received by him which had been cleared by him but not available for verification to have a fool proof case against the Indian exporter. During the interrogation it transpired that he was being paid a meagre amount of few lakhs for clearing the consignments and later destroying the same. He was induced to believe that he was badly cheated since the financial gains made by the Indian exporters were colossal and made at his risk and cost. Since the amount he received for his maltrade practices was nothing and he would have got colossal amount of few crores by way of reward had he acted as informer to the whole racket. To the surprise of the interrogators he developed a false belief that he could still act as informer and tendered a confessional statement giving graphic accounts of each consignment from the day one till the operations of the syndicate were busted by the Mumbai Customs Preventive Commissionerate. The sleuth of the Indian Customs returned triumphantly after a rich haul in the form of clinching corroborative evidence.

Appendix-A

Drug Law Enforcement - A Profile

National Policy on Narcotic Drugs and Psychotropic Substances is based on the Directive Principles contained in Article 47 of the Indian Constitution which directs that the 'State shall endeavor to bring about prohibition of the consumption, except for medicinal purposes, of intoxicating drugs injurious to health'.

The government's policy on the subject, which flows from the above said constitutional provision, is also guided by the international conventions on the subject. India is a signatory to :

- 1961 Single Convention in Narcotic Drugs as amended by the 1972 Protocol.
- Convention on Psychotropic Substances 1971.

United Nations Convention against Illicit Traffic in Narcotic Drugs and Psychotropic Substances, 1988.

The broad legislative policy in the matter is contained in the three Central Acts, viz. Drugs and Cosmetics Act, 1940. The Narcotic Drugs and Psychotropic Substances Act, 1985, and the Prevention of Illicit Traffic in Narcotic Drugs and Psychotropic Substances Act, 1988. The responsibility of drug abuse control, which is a central function, is carried out through a number of Ministries, Departments and Organizations. These include Ministry of Finance, Department of Revenue, which is having the nodal co-ordination role as administrators of the Narcotic Drugs and Psychotropic Substances Act, 1985, and the Prevention of Illicit Traffic in Narcotic Drugs and Psychotropic Substances Act, 1988.

The Narcotics Drugs and Psychotropic Substances Act, 1985, which came into effect from the 14th November 1985 made an express provision for constituting a Central Authority for the purpose of exercising the powers and functions of the Central Government under the Act. In exercise of the powers, the "Narcotics Control Bureau" was constituted with Headquarters at Delhi with effect from the 17th March 1986. The Bureau, subject to the supervision and control the Central Government, exercises the powers and functions of the Central Government for taking measures with respect to:

Co-ordination of actions by various offices, State Governments and other authorities under the NDPS Act, Customs Act, Drugs and Cosmetics Act and any other law for the time being in force in connection with the enforcement provisions of the NDPS Act, 1985.

- Implementation of the obligation in respect of counter measures against illicit traffic under the various international conventions and protocols that are in force at present or which may be ratified or acceded to by India in future.
- Assistance to concerned authorities in foreign countries and concerned international organizations to facilitate coordination and universal action for prevention and suppression of illicit traffic in these drugs and substances.
- Coordination of actions taken by the other concerned Ministries, Departments and Organizations in respect of matters relating to drug abuse.

While the overall coordination in the drug control matter is the function of the Narcotics Control Bureau, Department of Revenue, and various Departments/Organizations. The licensing functions for the Narcotics Commissioner under the Department of Revenue, the Drug Controllers and Excise Commissioners of the State/Union Territories performs medicinal and scientific purposes. They also have enforcement powers for dealing with complaints and detecting contravention.

The health, treatment and hospitalization facilities are the responsibility of the Ministry of Health and Family Welfare and Health Department of the States/Union Territories. They also administer the Drugs and Cosmetics Act, 1940, which has an important bearing on licensing and regulation in respect of Psychotropic Substances. Public welfare aspects of prevention of addiction and de-addiction efforts, public education for demand reduction and rehabilitation and social reintegration of the addicts are the responsibilities of the Ministry of Welfare and the Welfare Departments of the States/Union Territories who operate mainly through the non-governmental social welfare organizations. General enforcement of the provision of the NDPS Act, 1985 are looked after by various other enforcement agencies like Customs and Central Excise, State Police, Economic Intelligence Bureau, Central Bureau of Investigation etc. Para military forces like BSF, CRPF, Coast Guards etc. are also required to play an important role in tackling smuggling of drugs.

A network has been established all over the country by designating a senior officer of the multi-disciplinary enforcement agency for operational coordination on drug related matters.

Role of Narcotics Control Bureau

The NDPS Act empowers a number of Central and State Government enforcement Agencies to enforce the provisions of the Act. In order to maintain an effective coordination among the agencies, the Government of India created a Central Bureau called the Narcotics Control Bureau in the Ministry of Finance, on 17th March 1986. Apart from playing the role of coordinator amongst the various agencies, the officers of the Narcotics Control Bureau are also empowered to exercise the enforcement provisions under the NDPS Act.

The Narcotics Control Bureau is the apex-coordinating agency. It also functions as an enforcement agency through its field units located at Bombay, Delhi, Calcutta, Madras, Varanasi, Jodhpur, Chandigarh, Jammu, Ahmedabad, Imphal and Tiruvananthapuram which are considered to be sensitive from the point of view of trafficking.

The Zonal Units collect intelligence and work in close cooperation with the Customs and other law enforcement agencies. The Narcotics Control Bureau strives to promote inter-agency cooperation in India and abroad and implements the provisions of various International Conventions relating to drug abuse and illicit drug trafficking, inter alia, liaisoning with International agencies, such as Interpol, Customs Cooperation Council, HM Customs & Excise of UK, DEA of USA, RCMP of Canada, RILO Hong Kong, SAARC and enforcement agencies of various other countries. All cases with international ramifications are reported to the concerned agencies with a request to pass on and cause necessary inquiries in the concerned countries. In turn the NCB through suitable agency located in India is investigated cases referred to by them.

Role of Other Enforcement Agencies

The role of various enforcement agencies is complimentary to each other. The Central Bureau of Narcotics headed by Narcotics Commissioner of India supervises the control system over licit cultivation of poppy and production of opium, India happens to be the only licit exporter of opium in the world. The State Policy has concurrent powers of enforcement, and several states, particularly Maharashtra, Tamil Nadu, Gujarat, Uttar Pradesh, Madhya Pradesh and North Eastern States have taken initiative to strengthen Anti-Narcotics work by setting up dedicated cells for narcotics.

The major responsibility for controlling street level peddling and trafficking including its interfaces with transit traffic falls upon the state enforcement agencies, particularly the Police. The major responsibility for controlling the transit traffic along the land borders falls on the BSF and Customs anti-smuggling formations. At the seaports, there is major presence of Customs and the Coast Guard. NCB is a catalytic agent of harmonious multi-disciplinary process of imparting dynamism in the overall Drug Situation in India.

It is a well-known fact that narcotic trafficking and abuse is today a worldwide phenomenon and almost all countries of the world are affected by the onslaught of the narcotics problem either as source regions or as transit regions or as markets for narcotic drugs.

India's narcotic problem arises pre-dominantly from its proximity to the two major opiate producing regions which flank the country on either side, namely, the Golden Crescent (Pakistan, Afghanistan, Iran) in the west and the Golden Triangle (Myanmar, Thailand, and Laos) on the east. Nepal also is a traditional source of cannabis, both herbal and resinous. Further, being a licit producer of raw opium used for medicinal and research purposes (India is the only such country), there is scope for some leakage from the licit to the illicit channel despite stringent controls. Some reports of domestic manufacture of brown sugar have, of late, caused alarm. With the growing liberalization of commerce there is an ever-increasing danger of exploitation of trade channels for narcotics trafficking as has been experienced the world over.

Frequent operations have been initiated to destroy illicit cultivation of Cannabis and Opium in various parts of the country primarily in the areas of Chakrata and Uttarkashi in UP, Arunachal Pradesh, Manipur and Mizoram in the north-east, and Idukki District of Kerala and the adjacent Kodaikanal area of Tamil Nadu besides Andhra Pradesh and West Bengal. Besides large quantities of drugs name Opium, Cannabis, Hashish, Methaqualone, Heroin and Acetic Anhydride a precursor chemical used in the illicit manufacture of Heroin have been seized by the Narcotics Control Bureau and other law enforcement agencies.

Strategy

The Government of India in order to exercise strict control over narcotics drugs and psychotropic substances in India in the manner envisaged in the United Nations Conventions, consolidated the erstwhile principal Acts, namely, the Opium Act, 1857, the Opium Act, 1978 and the Dangerous Drugs Act, 1930 and enacted the Narcotic Drugs and Psychotropic Substances Act, 1985. The NDPS Act provides for stringent provisions for control and regulations of narcotics drugs and psychotropic substances besides providing for the forfeiture of property derived from, or used in, illicit traffic in narcotic drugs and psychotropic substances. The penal provisions under the Act are adequate to meet the challenges of well-organized gangs and smugglers.

One of the significant deterrent to the drug traffickers is the provision authorizing to freeze or seize and forfeit any illegally acquired property or asset of any description derived from or used in illicit trafficking of drugs. Such properties even in the name of relative or any other person can be freezed and forfeited and the burden of proof that the property is not illegally acquired lies on the person affected.

A detailed mechanism has been evolved in order to have a coordinated strategy against the evil of narcotics trafficking and abuse. At the Cabinet level, the Ministry of Home Affairs has evolved a scheme of periodic meetings with State Ministers/Secretaries and other high level functionaries. For this purpose, the States have been divided Zone-wise. Narcotics are frequently discussed agenda item in these meetings, particularly in respect of vulnerable states.

Taking a holistic view of the problem, a Narcotics Coordination Committee of Secretaries has been set up by the Government and the Ministries concerned with demand reduction as well as supply control are represented through their secretaries. At the field level, a Coordination Committee consisting of Heads of Central Enforcement Agencies and Enforcement Agencies of sensitive states has been set up by Narcotics Control Bureau. Quarterly meetings are held under the chairmanship of Director General, Narcotics Control Bureau. The performance of the agencies is reviewed in these meetings and intelligence is also exchanged.

Following the above pattern, various State Governments have also established a similar mechanism for coordination of their anti-narcotics efforts. Coordination; meetings are being held periodically at the Central and State level to review the working of enforcement agencies and to exchange intelligence on drug trafficking.

Coordination

There are several enforcement agencies dealing with narcotics and economic intelligence such as the Directorate General of Revenue Intelligence, Directorate of Enforcement, the Directorate General of Investigation of Income Tax and Central Economic Intelligence Bureau. With the Revenue Secretary having assumed direct charge of narcotics matters without any other intermediate level, coordination with all agencies has become easy and spontaneous. Interconnected crimes are now being investigated in a coordinated manner by different agencies. Cooperation with other agencies such as Central Bureau of Investigation and Intelligence Bureau has become easier, adequate and immediate. With Central Bureau of Narcotics, Narcotics Control Bureau and Directorate of Enforcement reporting directly to Secretary (Revenue) it has been possible to achieve extremely effective and coordinated approach to interconnected issues and expeditious decision making. Coordination with State Governments including at the level of Chief Ministers, Chief Secretaries and DGP's has become very effective.

Periodical coordination meetings are held with the representatives of the various Ministries, Organizations, State Governments dealing with drug law enforcement and drug related issues. The Government of India has also constituted a High Level Committee to undertake comprehensive review of the present arrangements for dealing with various aspects of the drug abuse problem.

International Co-operation

Keeping in view the spirit of the 1988 UN Convention against Illicit Traffic in Narcotic Drugs and Psychotropic Substances, India has been endeavoring to enter into bilateral agreements with like-minded countries in the matter of combating illicit traffic in drugs. So far, the bilateral agreements have been signed with the following countries :

1. United States of America (March, 1990)
2. Mauritius (January, 1990)
3. Afghanistan (August, 1990)
4. Russian Federation (January, 1993)
5. Myanmar (March, 1993)
6. Zambia (October, 1993)
7. U.A.E, (January, 1994)

An agreement on investigation and prosecution of crime and tracing, restraint and confiscation of the proceeds and instruments of crime (including crimes involving currency transfers) and terrorists fund was signed with the Government of United Kingdom in the year 1992. Besides, India has entered into MOUs with USA in May, 1984, with Iran in April, 1995 and Egypt in 1995.

India and Pakistan have a bilateral arrangement under which a committee to control drug trafficking and smuggling meets to discuss the various issues relating to drug trafficking and smuggling at senior levels.

During the year 1993, India ratified the SAARC Convention on Narcotic Drugs and Psychotropic Substances, which entered into force with effect from 15th September, 1993. This convention resembles the UN Convention against Illicit Traffics of Narcotics Drugs and Psychotropic Substances, 1988 in many aspects. India has signed extradition treaties, mutual legal assistance agreements and other specific agreements to combat terrorism and organized crimes, etc. Extradition treaties exist with Canada, UK, Netherlands, Belgium, Nepal, Bhutan and USA.

Mutual Legal Assistance Treaties have been signed with UK, Canada, Turkey and Switzerland. The agreements with Russian Federation, Bulgaria, Egypt, and Romania are aimed at combating international terrorism, organized crime, and illegal economic activities and include illicit trafficking in narcotic drugs and psychotropic substances.

Controlled Delivery Operations

Controlled delivery technique is an investigative tool aimed at nabbing the persons who employ others to act as drug couriers on their behalf. This technique can be employed successfully with mutual cooperation and assistance of drug law enforcement agencies of two or more countries. The Narcotics Control Bureau as India's nodal agency for narcotics law enforcement, has undertaken Controlled Delivery operations with a number of countries from time to time both on its own initiative or when suitable cases are brought to its notice by other enforcement agencies.

Precursors Control

Controls on precursor chemicals were first imposed in 1988 under Section 11 of the Customs Act, 1962 in the nature of checks on movement of Acetic Anhydride within specified inland area, 100 kms. on the Indo-Myanmar border and 50 kms. on the Indo-Pak border.

Acetic Anhydride is an essential precursor chemical used in the manufacture of Heroin and also Methaqualone. In order to check its diversion for misuse and export potential to neighboring Heroin manufacturing countries, this has been brought under strict restrictions of NDPS Act since 15.4.93. A multi-pronged strategy has been evolved to check its diversion both by enforcement efforts and by increasing awareness by taking the concerned industry into confidence.

The Government imposed more stringent controls in conformity with Article 12 of the 1988 Convention on Illicit Trafficking in Drugs, by declaring Acetic Anhydride as a controlled substance under the NDPS Act. Under this law the regime of control and penalties is more rigorous (up to 10 years imprisonment) and it extends throughout the country and covers all associated activities from manufacture or import upto retail sales and end use. Daily accounts in prescribed format has to be maintained, movement has to be covered by consignment notes in prescribed format, returns have to be filed, transit losses have to be promptly reported to designated officials etc.

In November, 1993, Government imposed further restrictions by bringing Acetic Anhydride on the negative list of import under Duty Exemption Entitlement Certificate (DEEC) scheme linked with export of finished goods. These measures caused considerable upset to legitimate international trading in liberalized economy, but the Government pushed ahead with these strong measures in wider interest. The Government has also declared N-Acetylanthranilic Acid as a controlled substance with effect from 24.10.94.

Pre-export Authorization in respect of Ephedrine

Ephedrine, which is a precursor, chemical included in Table 1 of the 1988 UN Convention against Illicit Traffic in Narcotic Drugs and Psychotropic Substances, was brought under the pre-export authorization. The Directorate General of Foreign Trade issued a Public Notice on 2nd January, 1996 according to which the above said chemical can be exported only after obtaining a 'No Objection Certificate' from the Narcotics Commissioner of India, Gwalior.

Import/Export Authorization Regime on Psychotropic substances

The NDPS Rules had three schedules notifying Narcotic Drugs and Psychotropic Substances according to their abuse potentiality and their medicinal use. These Rules specified these drugs or psychotropic substances in different categories. Some of such drugs and psychotropic substances (notified in Schedule II and Schedule III of the Rules) can be exported/imported after obtaining special export/import authorization/filing of declaration. Even after notifying these drugs/substances, there were still some psychotropic substances, which though included in the schedule of the NDPS Act, were not in schedules of the NDPS Rules, with the result that there was no control on their import/export. Government of India has deleted Schedule II and Schedule III of the NDPS Rules. The effect of this notification is that except the narcotic drugs and psychotropic substances notified in Schedule I of the NDPS Rules that are prohibited items, all the psychotropic substances that are specified in the schedule of NDPS Act, can be exported/imported only against an export/import license issued by the Narcotics Commissioner of India.

Constitution of Special Courts

For speedy trials of the accused facing charges under NDPS Act 1985 the special courts are established in the states which are facing the major problems of drug abuse as given below in addition to existing 35 Spl. Courts which are sanctioned and are in the process of being constituted.

S.No.	*Name of State / Union Territory*	*Number of Courts*
1.	Goa	1
2.	Maharashtra	15
3.	Sikkim	1
4.	Manipur	4
5.	Meghalaya	5
6.	Nagaland	8
7.	Tripura	1
8.	West Bengal	4
9.	Tamil Nadu	6
10.	Rajasthan	1
11.	Delhi	10
12.	Kerala	14
		70
		+ 35*
	Total	105

* Being constituted.

Preventive Detention under Narcotic Offences

This is an Act to provide for detention in certain cases for the purpose of preventing illicit traffic in Narcotic Drugs and Psychotropic Substances.

The NDPS Act, 1985 provides for deterrent punishments for drug trafficking offenses. Even though offenses under the Act are non-bailable by virtue of the quantum of punishment, due offenders were being released on bail on technical grounds, since the proper provisions of the Act were not cited.

The Cabinet Committee constituted for combating drug traffic and to prevent drug abuse, recommended that additional legislative measures could be in the form of prevention detention scheme covering all aspects of drug trafficking.

Accordingly as recommendation of the Cabinet Sub-Committee a Preventive Ordinance title "The Prevention of Illicit Traffic in Narcotic Drugs and Psychotropic Substances Ordinance, 1988 (PITNDPS) was promulgated by the President on 4th July 1988. This was subsequently made into a law in August.

Preventive detention is not a substitute for the normal laws nor is it intended to be used in lieu of such laws. This additional weapon in the armoury of the law enforcement agencies is aimed at organized trafficking in drugs. While specific contravention of NDPS Act will continue to be dealt with by prosecutions in court, some situations may arise even in such cases where preventive detention may be found necessary to prevent the continued illegal activities of the persons concerned.

1. Organizers, financiers and their agents who organize things from behind the scene: These persons do not normally handle Narcotic Drugs or Psychotropic Substances themselves nor do they directly engage in illicit trafficking. They do not give any written instructions, and the carriers and others who actually work on their behalf are afraid to give any evidence against them. However, the intelligence gathered over a period of time and the circumstantial evidence would be adequate to convince independent authorities like the Advisory Boards that these persons have been organizing or financing illicit trafficking and should, therefore, be detained to prevent them from continuing their prejudicial activities.

2. Habitual or organized illicit traffickers caught red handed with narcotics drugs and psychotropic substances to be detained pending prosecution: These persons though caught red handed and proceeded against, continue to indulge in their prejudicial activities whenever released on bail. They are also able to tamper with witnesses and the evidence and thereby weaken the prosecution cases frustrating the ends of justice. However, in order to ensure that detentions of these persons are done on a selective basis and confined to cases involving organized illicit trafficking, a minimum quantity limit has been specified as detailed below :

(i)	Opium	10 kg.
(ii)	Morphine	500 gms.
(iii)	Heroin	500 gms.
(iv)	Cocaine	250 gms.
(v)	Ganja	50 gms.
(vi)	Charas	10 kg.

(vii) In cases involving psychotropic substances preventive detention may be resorted to keeping in view of the commercial nature of activity.

However, in cases of repeat habitual offenders, the quantity limit will not be the guiding factor.

3. Licensed cultivators indulging in embezzlement of opium, or undertaking excess cultivation beyond the condonable limit laid down by the Government from time to time, the persons indulging in illicit cultivation of opium poppy/cannabis, the detention will be for the period required for completion of investigation/prosecution proceedings in a court of law and not necessarily for the maximum period prescribed in the Prevention of Illicit Traffic in Narcotics Drugs and Psychotropic Substances Ordinance, 1988.

4. An individual detained under PITNDPS Act, 1988 can be detained for a maximum period of two years.

5. If the appropriate government has a reason to believe that person in respect of whom the detention order has been made has absconded or concealing himself so that the order cannot be executed, that Government may declare him absconder under Section 8 (a & b) of the Act.

In the case of persons absconding, the government may, by order, notify in the Official Gazette, or in daily national newspapers direct such person to appear before such officer at place/time as may be specified. If the person fails to do so without sufficient or reasonable cause, he shall be punishable with imprisonment upto to one year or with fine or both.

6. Central Government and each State Government shall consist of a Chairman and two other persons possessing specified qualifications and that appropriate Government shall make a reference to the Advisory Board within 5 weeks of date of detention of the person to enable the Advisory Board to offer its opinion, after due examination, as to whether there is sufficient cause for detention in terms of the PITNDPS Act, 1988.

Forfeiture of Properties

The drug trade in India and indeed throughout the world is dominated by organized crime. Criminals operate for the sole purpose of financial gains and power that goes with it. Illicit trade in drugs generates large profits and wealth. This not only hampers and affects legitimate trade and commerce but also results in links with other crimes. Narco-crime and Narco-terrorism are not new words for investigating officers of drug enforcement agencies. For effectively containing the menace of drug trafficking, the Government of India has accordingly amended the Narcotics Drugs and Psychotropic Substances Act, 1985.

Amendment of the Law

A Bill was introduced in Parliament on 29th November 1988 to strengthen the NDPS Act. One of the major reasons for amendment was to provide for forfeiture of property and prescribe a detailed procedure for the same. The NDPS (Amendment) Act, 1988 came into force on 29th May, 1989. Under the Amendment Law, a new Chapter V-A: "Forfeiture of property derived from or used in Illicit Traffic was incorporated. Thus, the NDPS Act 1985 as amended has now twin enforcement programme containing elaborate provisions for prosecution of drug related offenses and more importantly for forfeiture of assets of drug traffickers.

Reasons for amendment — Background

The international and national background resulting in formulation of law on forfeiture of property are given below :

International Level

The Commission on Narcotic Drugs of United Nation, in February, 1983 adopted a resolution on forfeiture of proceeds of drugs. It was felt that depriving drug traffickers of their proceeds specially money power would be an effective means of reducing illicit traffic in drugs. Ultimately, in 1988 United Nation Plenipotentiary Conference providing for identification, tracing, freezing, seizure and confiscation of property related to drugs adopted a new convention.

National Level

India is a signatory to 1988 convention and by virtue of Article 253 of Indian Constitution is under obligation to implement the same. In order to implement the provisions of the Convention, the Government of India amended the NDPS Act, in 1988 to incorporate suitable provisions for forfeiture of illicit property of drug traffickers.

Salient Features

The salient features of forfeiture of property are as follows :

Application

The Law relating to forfeiture of property is applicable to certain specified class of persons and briefly, these persons are :

(i) Those convicted for an offence punishable for a term of five years or more under the Act.

(ii) Those convicted for similar offense by a competent Court outside India.

(iii) Those detained under the PITNDPS Act, 1988 or J&K PITNDPS Act, 1988 provided their detention is not set aside.

(iv) Certain relatives or associates of persons mentioned in (i) to (iii) above.

Limitation

The forfeiture provisions apply to all property acquired before a period of six years from the date on which he was charged for on offense relating to illicit traffic in drug.

Trends in seizure of Narcotic Drugs and Psychotropic Substances in India is quite alarming as would be evident from the seizure figures of past few years as below

Hashish

YEAR	1996	1997	1998	1999	2000	2001	2002	2003 (upto 7/03)
QTY.(KG)	6520	3285	10106	3391	5041	5664	3300	983
CASES	2593	2223	2193	2500	2078	2117	2121	784

Methaqualone

YEAR	1996	1997	1998	1999	2000	2001	2002	2003 (upto 7/03)
QTY.(K.G)	2212	1740	2257	474	1095	2024	11130	–
CASES	405	207	114	8	31	8	7	–

Number of cases has drastically declined from 405 in 1996 to 7 cases in 2002. The decline is attributed to the fact that clandestine manufacture activities have shifted to other West Asian countries since 1998.

Acetic Anhydride

YEAR	1996	1997	1998	1999	2000	2001	2002	2003 (upto 7/03)
QTY.(ltr)	4627	8311	6197	2963	1337	8589	3288	4
CASES	14	12	9	7	14	8	4	1

Acetic Anhydride is a precursor chemical for the manufacture of heroin. Because of the strict control on the chemical, there is definite decline in smuggling of the Acetic Anhydride through the land border, in last two years.

Opium

YEAR	1996	1997	1998	1999	2000	2001	2002	2003 (upto /03)
QTY.(KG)	2875	3221	2031	1635	2684	2533	1867	690
CASES	977	1333	954	927	1257	1205	1167	359

Most of the seizures were affected in the adjoining poppy growing areas in Uttar Pradesh, Madhya Pradesh and Rajasthan. Large quantities of poppy husk were seized in Punjab, Rajasthan, Madhya Pradesh and Uttar Pradesh.

Heroin

YEAR	1996	1997	1998	1999	2000	2001	2002	2003 (upto 7/03)
QTY.(KG)	1257	1332	655	861	1240	889	884	377
CASES	3043	2990	3095	2937	2841	3891	4328	1862

The seizure trends in Heroin also show decline. This is mainly attributed to the fact that South West Asian Heroin, which used to figure significantly in our seizure, is now invariably moving to Europe through the Balkan and CIS routes.

National Drug Enforcement Statistics as Reported upto 31/07/03

Year		1999	2000	2001	2002	2003
1. Seizures of Various Drugs in Kg. with No. of Cases						
Opium	Seizures	1635	2684	2533	1867	690
	Cases	927	1257	1205	1167	359
Morphine	Seizures	36	39	26	66	23
	Cases	125	142	146	148	87
Heroin	Seizures	861	1240	889	884	377
	Cases	2937	2841	3891	4328	1862
Ganja	Seizures	40113	100056	86929	88137	28711
	Cases	6518	6073	7613	3687	2123
Hashish	Seizures	3391	5041	5664	3300	983
	Cases	2500	2078	2117	2121	784
Cocaine	Seizures	1	0.350	2	2	1
	Cases	4	5	10	5	4
Methaqualone	Seizures	474	1095	2024	11130	—
	Cases	8	31	8	7	
Ephedrine	Seizures	-	426	930	126	4258
	Cases	-	8	5	4	6
L.S.D	Seizures	240	0	0	0	
(Sq. Paper)	Cases	3	8	0	0	
Acetic Anhydride	Seizures	2963	1337	8589	3288	4
(in Ltrs.)	Cases	7	14	8	4	1
Amphetamine	Seizures	~	3	0	0	—
	Cases	~	11	0	0	—

2. Person arrested

	1999	2000	2001	2002	2003
(a) Nos. of person arrested including Foreigners	13490	15065	16315	12318	5740
(b) Nos. of Foreigners Arrested	92	92	133	172	54

3. Action taken against persons involved in drug traficking

	1999	2000	2001	2002	2003
(a) Nos. of person prosecuted	10841	19162	12358	12496	3329
(b) Nos. of persons convicted	2891	4447	3419	5310	1196
(c) Nos. of persons acquitted	4632	5416	4712	5089	1111

4. Action taken under PITNDPS (NDPS) Act, 1988

	1999	2000	2001	2002	2003
Nos. of detention orders issued under PITNDPS Act, 1988	53	73	61	65	8
Nos. detained	44	73	46	63	8

NATIONAL DRUG ENFORCEMENT STATISTICS (PROVISIONAL AS ON 31/08/98)

Year		1994	1995	1996	1997	1998
1. Seizures of Various Drugs in Kg. with No. of Cases						
Opium	Seizures	2256	1339	2875	3221	997
	Cases	1171	871	977	1333	393
Morphine	Seizures	51	4	4	76	14
	Cases	145	35	37	75	28
Heroin	Seizures	1011	1678	1257	1329	310
	Cases	3331	3236	3043	2990	929
Ganja	Seizures	187896	121873	62992	80866	30904
	Cases	6827	5737	5833	7062	2254
Hashish	Seizures	6992	3629	6520	3285	7379
	Cases	2672	2691	2593	2223	631
Cocaine	Seizures	1.58	40	3	24	0
	Cases	6	6	8	6	1
Methaqualone	Seizures	45319	20485	2212	1740	666
	Cases	457	196	405	207	103
Phenobarbital	Seizures	-	~	—	—	—
	Cases	-	~	—	—	—
L.S.D	Seizures	256	113	1285	—	27
(Sq. Paper)	Cases	—	1	7	—	0
Acetic Anhydride	Seizures	47740	9282	4627	8311	6142
(in Ltrs.)	Cases	40	26	14	12	5
2. Person arrested						
(a) Nos. of person arrested including Foreigners		15452	14673	13554	14565	4740
(b) Nos. of Foreigners Arrested		136	148	130	99	35
3. Action taken against persons involved in drug trafficking						
(a) Nos. of person prosecuted		9154	12918	12198	13203	8932
(b) Nos. of persons convicted		1245	2456	2963	2796	1331
(c) Nos. of persons acquitted		3156	3914	6102	4944	3740
4. Action taken under PITNDPS (NDPS) Act, 1988						
Nos. of detention orders issued under PITNDPS Act, 1988		156	111	80	82	27
Nos. detained		123	89	67	68	20

Narcotic Drugs Seized by DRI from 01.10.2000 to 31.12.2000 at a Glance

Name of Drug	No. of Cases	Qty. in Kgs.	No. of persons arrested		
			Indians	Foreigners	Total
Heroin	7	36.330	13	—	13
Ganja	14	4331.240	15	—	15
Ephedrine	1	100.000	—	—	—
Charas	3	99.700	—	—	—
Mandrax	2	613.200	5	—	5
Hashish	4	306.444	2	—	2
Opium	1	5.685	—	—	—
Total	32		35		35

Narcotic Drugs Seized by DRI From 01.01.2001 to 31.12.2001 at a Glance

Name of Drug	No. of Cases	Qty. in Kgs.	No. of persons arrested		
			Indians	Foreigners	Total
Heroin	18	173.483	28	5	33
Morphine	1	0.950	—	1	1
Mandrax	2	877.250	3	—	3
Ganja	13	16996.850	18	—	18
Hashish	3	91.000	—	—	—
Total	37		49	6	55

NARCOTIC DRUGS SEIZED BY DRI From 01.01.2002 to 31.12.2002 at a Glance

Name of Drug	No. of Cases	Qty. in Kgs.	No. of persons arrested		
			Indians	Foreigners	Total
Heroin	14	119.475	21	2	23
Morphine	1	18.690	*	—	*
Mandrax/ Mathaqualone	4	7788.500	11	1	12
Ganja	6	7140.200	7	—	7
Hashish	5	1186.500	2	2	4
Prednisolone (Steroid)	1	10.000	—	—	—
Total	31		41	5	46

*Three persons arrested in the seizure case of Morphine of 18.690 Kgs. effected by DRI Surat on 01.07.2002, have been included in the arrested list of seizure cases of Heroin as those persons have been arrested with Heroin in addition.

Narcotic Drugs Seized by DRI
From 01.01.2003 to 31.12.2003 at a Glance

Name of Drug	*No. of Cases*	*Qty. in Kgs.*	*No. of persons arrested*		
			Indians	*Foreigners*	*Total*
Heroin	8	56.050	10	3	13
Ganja	9	3154.000	9	—	9
Cannabis	1	45.000	—	—	—
Hashish	4	1219.100	3	—	3
Ephedrine	1	2024.000	2	—	2
Methaqualone	1	58.7	—	—	—
Tidigesic Injection	1	10900 ampoules of 2 ml	—	—	—
Total	25	6556.85+ 10900 ampoules of 2 ml. each	24	3	27

Comparative Performance in Respect of Major Narcotics Seizures in India

(IN KGS.)

Name of drug and year	*Seizures by Customs and Central Excise*		*Seizure by CBN*		*Seizure by other Central Agencies*		*Seizures by DRI*		*Seizures by NCB*		*Total Qty. seized in India (all agencies incl. State agencies*
	Qty.	%	**Qty.**	%	**Qty.**	%	**Qty.**	%	**Qty.**	%	
Hashish											
1994	1193	18.27	—	0	446	6.83	1340	20.52	261	4.00	6532
1995	850	23.43	—	0	504	13.89	130	3.59	27	0.74	3629
1996	767	11.77	7	0.11	142	2.18	3627	55.63	135	2.07	6520
1997	572	17.44	206	6.28	249	7.59	25	0.77	157	4.79	3281
1998	6632	65.63	37	0.37	882	8.73	94	0.93	896	8.87	10106
1999	862	25.42	16	0.47	22	0.65	702	20.70	101	2.98	3391
2000	1739	34.50	15	0.29	,–	0	646	12.81	213	4.22	5041
2001	2455	48.00	12	1.00	10	1.00	51+40	1	177	4.00	5164+40
2002	—	—		—	—	—	750.500	42.34	1022	56.53	1772.5
2003	—	—		—	—	—	4	1.23	321	98.76	325+657

Source: NCB REPORT (JULY. 2003)

Comparative Performance in Respect of Major Narcotics Seizures in India

(IN KGS.)

Name of drug and year	*Seizures by Customs and Central Excise*		*Seizure by CBN*		*Seizure by other Central Agencies*		*Seizures by DRI*		*Seizures by NCB*		*Total Qty. seized in India (all agencies incl. State agencies)*
	Qty.	*%*	*Qty.*	*%*	*Qty.*	*%*	*Qty.*	*%*	*Qty.*	*%*	
Ganja (Marijuana)											
1994	19249	13.29	.155	0.11	713	0.50	1170	0.81	2944	2.04	144900
1995	6754	5.55	52	0.05	2073	1.70	1633	1.34	462	0.38	121873
1996	1058	1.68	48	0.08	2569	4.08	111	0.18	650	1.04	62992
1997	2568	3.18	66	0.09	3464	4.29	2508	3.10	3022	3.74	80886
1998	12706	18.63	461	0.68	3893	5.71	7773	11.40	651	0.96	68221
1999	837	2.08	31	0.07	485	1.20	4806	11.98	3362	8.38	40113
2000	3042	3.03	14	0	364	0.36	4022+209	4.21	543	0.54	100056+209
2001	3685	5.00	137	1.00	809	1.00	11937+ 5059.85	16	474	1.00	75943+5059.85
2002	1006	9.16	18	01.64	3526	32.13	6205.100	56.55	486	4.42	10971.100
2003	528	4.52	40	0.34	702	6.02	2913	24.98	2578	22.10	6761+4900

Source: NCB REPORT (JULY. 2003)

Comparative Performance in Respect of Major Narcotics Seizures in India

(IN KGS.)

Name of drug and year	Seizures by Customs and Central Excise		Seizure by CBN		Seizure by other Central Agencies		Seizures by DRI		Seizures by DRI		Total Qty. seized in India (all agencies incl. State agencies)
	Qty.	%	Qty.	%	Qty.	%	Qty.	%	Qty.	%	
Methaqualone											
1994	4897	15.07	—	0	—	0	19782	33.17	676	2.08	32509
1995	205	1.00	—	0	—	0	14099	68.83	1064	5.20	20485
1996	4	0.18	—	0	—	0	1765	79.80	—	—	2212
1997	—	—	11	0.64	—	0	595	34.20	—	—	1740
1998	421	18.66	4	0.18	—	0	1457	64.56	268	11.88	2257
1999	39	8.23	7	1.48	—	0	285	60.13	50	10.55	474
2000	—	0	—	0	—	0	709	64.75	295	26.94	1095
2001	—	—	—	—	—	—	396+481.25	20.00	1588	80.00	1984 + 481.25
2002	205	1.87	—	—	—	—	7788.500	71.05	2967	27.06	10960.500
2003	—	—	—	—	—	—	—	—	—	—	—
Heroin											
1994	138	15.24	14	1.55	172	18.99	6	0.67	96	10.60	906
1995	207	12.32	60	3.57	653	38,85	243	14.46	75	4.47	1681
1996	164	13.05	17	1.36	145	11.54	354	28.17	104	8.28	1257
1997	321	24.10	100	7.51	110	8.26	203	15.24	86	6.46	1332
1998	189	28.86	101	15.42	16	2.45	77	11.76	66	10.08	655
1999	205	23.80	33	3.83	42	4.88	41	4.76	301	34.96	861
2000	100	8.03	25	2	90	8.10	33	2.97	344	27.65	1240
2001	116	15	52	7.00	28	4.00	142+31.49	18.00	1978	25.00	813+31.49
2002	30	6.47	38	8.19	3	0.64	85.550	18.45	307	66.22	463.55
2003	28	7.42	1	0.26	1	0.26	29	7.69	102	27.02	161+216

Source: NCB REPORT (JULY, 2003).

Appendix-B

Prices of Gold in the London Metal Market (Per Troy oz in US $)

Year	*US$*	*Year*	*US$*	*Year*	*US$*	*Year*	*US$*	*Year*	*US$*
1833	20.65	1868	20.65	1898	20.71	1933	26.33	1968	38.69
1834	20.65	1869	20.65	1899	20.66	1934	34.69	1969	41.09
1835	20.65	1870	20.65	1900	20.68	1935	34.84	1970	35.94
1836	20.65	1871	20.65	1901	20.71	1936	34.87	1971	40.80
1837	20.65	1872	20.66	1902	20.69	1937	34.79	1972	58.16
1838	20.65	1873	20.66	1903	20.67	1938	34.85	1973	97.32
1839	20.65	1874	20.66	1904	20.68	1939	34.42	1974	159.26
1840	20.65	1875	20.66	1905	20.64	1940	33.85	1975	161.02
1841	20.65	1871	20.65	1906	20.62	1941	33.85	1976	124.84
1842	20.65	1872	20.66	1907	20.66	1942	33.85	1977	147.71
1843	20.65	1873	20.66	1908	20.67	1943	33.85	1978	193.22
1844	20.65	1874	20.66	1909	20.68	1944	33.85	1979	306.68
1845	20.65	1875	20.66	1910	20.64	1945	34.71	1980	612.56
1846	20.65	1876	20.65	1911	20.74	1946	34.71	1981	460.03
1847	20.65	1877	20.66	1912	20.65	1947	34.71	1982	375.67
1848	20.65	1878	20.66	1913	20.64	1948	34.71	1983	424.35
1849	20.65	1879	20.66	1914	20.72	1949	31.69	1984	360.38
1850	20.65	1880	20.66	1915	20.72	1950	34.72	1985	317.26
1851	20.65	1881	20.65	1916	20.72	1951	34.72	1986	367.66
1852	20.65	1882	20.66	1917	20.72	1952	34.60	1987	446.46
1853	20.65	1883	20.66	1918	20.72	1953	34.84	1988	436.94
1854	20.65	1884	20.66	1919	20.70	1954	35.04	1989	381.44
1855	20.65	1885	20.66	1920	20.68	1955	35.03	1990	383.51
1856	20.65	1886	20.65	1921	20.58	1956	34.99	1991	362.11
1857	20.65	1887	20.66	1922	20.66	1957	34.95	1992	343.82
1858	20.65	1888	20.66	1923	20.32	1958	35.10	1993	359.77
1859	20.65	1889	20.66	1924	20.69	1959	35.10	1994	384.00
1860	20.65	1890	20.66	1925	20.64	1960	35.27	1995	384.17
1861	20.65	1891	20.68	1926	20.63	1961	35.25	1996	387.77
1862	20.65	1892	20.68	1927	20.64	1962	35.23	1997	330.98
1863	20.65	1893	20.68	1928	20.66	1963	35.09	1998	294.24
1864	20.65	1894	20.66	1929	20.63	1964	35.10	1999	278.88
1865	20.65	1895	20.65	1930	20.65	1965	35.12	2000	279.78
1866	20.65	1896	20.71	1931	17.06	1966	35.13	2001	272.08
1867	20.65	1897	20.71	1932	20.69	1967	34.95	2002	310.35

Appendix-C

Prices of Gold in the India From 1925 to 2002
(Per 10 Grams in Rupees)

Year	*Rs.*	*Year*	*Rs.*	*Year*	*Rs.*
1925	18	1951	98	1977	573
1926	18	1952	76	1978	665
1927	18	1953	73	1979	937
1928	18	1954	77	1980	1330
1929	18	1955	79	1981	1700
1930	18	1956	90	1982	1645
1931	18	1957	90	1983	1800
1932	23	1958	95	1984	1975
1933	25	1959	102	1985	2130
1934	28	1960	111	1986	2140
1935	30	1961	119	1987	2570
1936	29	1962	120	1988	3130
1937	30	1963	97	1989	3140
1938	29	1964	108	1990	3200
1939	31	1965	123	1991	3466
1940	36	1966	144	1992	4334
1941	37	1967	NA	1993	4140
1942	44	1968	162	1994	4611
1943	51	1969	176	1995	4680
1944	52	1970	184	1996	5160
1945	62	1971	193	1997	4725
1946	83	1972	203	1998	4045
1947	88	1973	278	1999	4235
1948	95	1974	506	2000	4380
1949	94	1975	540	2001	4366
1950	99	1976	532	2002	5023

Courtesy: Bombay Bullion Association.

PROFITABILITY OF SMUGGING OF GOLD INTO INDIA

Period	*Price of Gold in Bombay (Rs. per 10 gms.)*	*Price of Gold in London (US$/tr.oz)*	*Hawala Conversion rate in Bombay (Rs./US$)*	*Price of Gold in London (in Rs.)*	*Add Incidental charges in London Price@ Rs. 40/- per 10 grams.*	*Profitability*
1996	5189.79	387.88	39.04	4868.42	4928.42	261.37
1997	4558.24	330.97	40.21	4278.62	4318.62	239.62
1998	.4178.64	294.02	42.34	4002.29	4042.29	136.35
1999	4330.55	279.22	44.76	4018.07	4058.07	272.48
2000	4519.85	279.78	47.09	4235.71	4275.71	244.14
2001	4466.73	272.08	48.56	4247.72	4287.72	179.01
2002*	5123.32	310.35	49.88	4976.90	5016.90	106.42
2003*						
Jan., 03	5709.72	353.72	49.18	5591.99	5631.99	77.73
Feb., 03	5794.34	362.86	48.40	5646.13	5686.13	108.22
Mar., 03	5453.89	343.28	48.91	5398.40	5438.40	15.49
April., 03	5153.33	325.45	48.62	5086.85	5126.85	26.48
May., 03	5575.31	358.17	48.25	5555.59	5595.59	–20.27

***Figures are provisional**

PROFITABILITY OF SMUGGING OF SILVER INTO INDIA (REPORT FOR THE MONTH OF MAY 2003)

Period	*Price of Silver in Bombay (Rs. per gms.)*	*Price of Silver in London (New Pense) per tr. oz)*	*Hawala Conversion rate in Bombay (Rs./UK.P)*	*Price of Silver in London (in Rs.)*	*Add Incidental charges in London Price@ Rs. 445/- per kg*	*Profitability*
1996	7291.90	334.81	60.32	6492.93	6937.93	353.97
1997	7002.02	299.74	65.02	6265.74	6710.74	291.28
1998	7998.97	335.94	69.92	7551.69	7996.69	2.28
1999	8026.17	324.12	72.23	7526.7	7971.70	54.47
2000	7997.81	328.20	71.27	7520.14	7965.15	32.66
2001	7419.25	304.84	70.09	6869.24	7314.24	105.01
2002*	7934.86	309.37	74.73	7432.83	7877.83	57.03
2003*						
Jan, 03	8151.96	298.65	79.25	7608.99	8053.99	97.96
Feb., 03	7958.57	289.23	79.16	7332.78	7777.78	180.79
March, 03	7814.72	287.24	47.23	7133.10	7578.10	236.63
April, 03	7796.67	284.22	77.05	7039.94	7484.94	311.73
May, 03	8005.63	292.90	78.58	7399.04	7844.04	161.58

***Figures are provisional**

Appendix-D

All India Seizures of Major Commodities

S.No.	*Name of the items*	*1999-00*	*2000-01*	*2001-02*	*2002-03*
(I)	Total value of seizures (Outright Smuggling)	1843.26	747.40	602.61	468.53
	Seizure of major commodities in respect of outright smuggling.				
	1. Gold	41.60	24.28	25.04	14.53
	2. Foreign currency	18.56	17.25	21.58	13.66
	3. Yarn and fabrics	34.88	55.24	47.88	22.45
	4. Electronic items	65.44	68.39	39.80	48.97
	5. Computer and computer parts	7.83	12.52	10.70	6.34
	6. Narcotic drugs	24.28	23.54	25.48	29.04
	7. Ball bearings	26.62	12.86	3.52	0.81
	8. Machinery and Machine parts	897.78	217.13	56.48	11.48
	9. Vessels/vehicles	355.86	70.23	44.66	47.48
	10. Miscellaneous	370.41	245.96	327.47	273.77
(II)	**Duty value of evasion cases**	**1772.17**	**456.46**	**1055.37**	**809.14**
	Major commodities in respect of duty evasion cases.				
	1 . Electronics	70.81	48.56	35.06	4.61
	2. Synthetic yarn and fabrics	167.53	23.81	93.92	22.12
	3. Machinery and Machine parts	158.98	90.74	340.24	34.73
	4. Misc. / Others	1374.85	293.35	586.15	747.68

Index